BE THE MAN

The Man Registry® Guide for Grooms

Chris Easter

ALPHA

A member of Penguin Group (USA) Inc.

ALPHA BOOKS

Published by the Penguin Group

Penguin Group (USA) Inc., 375 Hudson Street, New York, New York 10014, USA

Penguin Group (Canada), 90 Eglinton Avenue East, Suite 700, Toronto, Ontario M4P 2Y3, Canada (a division of Pearson Penguin Canada Inc.)

Penguin Books Ltd., 80 Strand, London WC2R 0RL, England

Penguin Ireland, 25 St. Stephen's Green, Dublin 2, Ireland (a division of Penguin Books Ltd.)

Penguin Group (Australia), 250 Camberwell Road, Camberwell, Victoria 3124, Australia (a division of Pearson Australia Group Pty. Ltd.)

Penguin Books India Pvt. Ltd., 11 Community Centre, Panchsheel Park, New Delhi—110 017, India

Penguin Group (NZ), 67 Apollo Drive, Rosedale, North Shore, Auckland 1311, New Zealand (a division of Pearson New Zealand Ltd.)

Penguin Books (South Africa) (Pty.) Ltd., 24 Sturdee Avenue, Rosebank, Johannesburg 2196, South Africa

Penguin Books Ltd., Registered Offices: 80 Strand, London WC2R 0RL, England

Copyright © 2012 by Christopher Easter

International Standard Book Number: 978-1-61564-131-4
Library of Congress Catalog Card Number: 2011910189

14   13   12   8   7   6   5   4   3   2   1

Interpretation of the printing code: The rightmost number of the first series of numbers is the year of the book's printing; the rightmost number of the second series of numbers is the number of the book's printing. For example, a printing code of 12-1 shows that the first printing occurred in 2012.

Printed in the United States of America

This book is dedicated to all of the men who choose to boldly step into the world of wedding planning. Also, to my wife—thanks for letting me have some fun with our wedding day.

Contents

Foreword

What would you say if I told you that one of my favorite movies of all time was a 1970's romance? Hold on—don't pull my "man card" just yet. The movie is *Rocky*. Sure there's an epic training montage and colossal fight at the end—but behind all that is the story of a down-and-out boxer who finds strength and support in the woman working in the neighborhood pet store. I want you to think about this as you go through the wedding-planning process. Your wedding and the tasks leading up to it can be what you want to make of it, and this book is stuffed with everything you need to know.

From your budget to your bachelor party, from rehearsal to reception, think of *Be the Man: The Man Registry® Guide for Grooms* as your Mickey. This book gives it to you straight and will help you formulate a winning strategy. Let's be honest—you might take a few shots and have to make some sacrifices, but that goes for most triumphant endeavors. Being the man means doing things you sometimes don't want, like picking flowers or switching out of a southpaw stance.

Throughout this book, you'll find much inspiration and guidance. The checklist and timeline in Chapter 3 is as sound as cracking a half-dozen raw eggs and dropping them down your gullet. In Chapter 10, you'll find out how to survive an outing in Las Vegas and how to put together co-ed bachelor(ette) parties if that's the route you want to go.

Of course, all this planning leads up to the big day. No, not a fight—your wedding. In your corner is your soon-to-be wife. And with this book, you two can stay on the same page from your first preparations to the final (wedding) bell. Can you hear the music? Are you getting pumped? This is your shot to throw the biggest celebration of your life with everyone who cares about you cheering for you.

As the big day approaches and everything begins to fly at you quickly, you might find that your legs get wobbly and your head spins. If you feel that you're goin' down, this book is gonna whisper in your ear. It's gonna say, "'Get up, you son of a bitch, 'cause Mickey loves you.'"

Congratulations!

—Steve Cooper, Hitched Media

Introduction

First things first: I want to commend you for having the courage to walk into a book store, stroll over to the wedding section, and pick up a copy of this book. I know it probably wasn't easy. Of course, you may have also received this book as a gift from a well-meaning fiancée or family member, which is also perfectly acceptable. So props to you for opening it up!

Now, do me a favor and forget about all your pre-conceived thoughts about men and wedding planning. The days of grooms being innocent bystanders in the planning process are long gone, and that's a great thing. Today's grooms are wedding-planning connoisseurs and are finding increasingly creative ways to leave a personal mark on their weddings. This doesn't mean that you have to become well-versed in the language of floral arrangements, nor does it mean you'll be accompanying your bride as she tries on dozens of gowns and frets over bridesmaid dress colors. On the contrary, there are literally hundreds of reasons why you, the *man,* can and should get excited about your role in planning your own wedding.

Right about now, you may be wondering what makes me an authority to advise you on planning your wedding. Good question. Three years ago, I and my two future brothers-in-law were knee-deep in the world of weddings. They had both recently tied the knot, and I was just starting down the road of planning my own wedding. Furthermore, we all had buddies who were also nervously treading into the murky waters of popping the question and getting engaged. As it turned out, there was one common thread that tied us all together: confusion and cluelessness.

We wanted to take a hands-on approach to the situation, but the resources available to us were extremely limited. Compared to the thousands of magazines, websites, blogs, TV programs, and movies aimed at the bride, there was essentially *zilch* out there to help educate the groom. Further complicating matters was the fact that the very few groom-oriented resources available were written by women! Heartbreaking, I know.

We decided to take matters into our own hands, and thus the concept for our website, TheManRegistry.com, was born. The site was created with the goal of guiding men through the wedding-planning process and showing guys that they, too, can have a little fun in the process.

Be the Man is the culmination of years of researching, blogging, and speaking on the topic of the groom's involvement in weddings. It's intended to give you the play-by-play of the wedding-planning months, answer lingering questions, and debunk age-old myths. In addition to the do's and don'ts, I also highlight some of the more offbeat methods of saving coin, getting along with your Bridezilla (err, fiancée), and surviving a wedding shower in one piece. And yes, to answer your question, there are chapters on how to wow your bride on the wedding night and plan your bachelor party. Look at it this way: your fiancée already has the traditional big book of all-things wedding. *Be the Man* is the dude's guide to wedding planning that focuses on only the stuff you need (and want) to know.

The book is broken into 16 chapters that roughly follow the timeline of events and checkpoints that will occur during your engagement all the way through the wedding day and night. Depending on where you are in planning and what type of wedding you're having, some chapters may not apply to you, so feel free to skip those. For example, if you're already engaged, you can skip Chapter 1, "Engagement Ring Shopping," and Chapter 2, "The Rules of Engagement." Similarly, if you're planning a small destination wedding, some chapters might not apply to you and your bride.

I wrote this book in the hopes that it will be a quick and simple read instead of a book you have to read for hours on a Sunday afternoon when you should be throwing a football outside or messing around in the garage. I encourage you to give the table of contents a quick scan right now and then come back to certain chapters as they become more relevant during your planning process.

Throughout the book, you'll find multiple sidebars designed to recap a main point in the chapter or give you a quick piece of topical advice. These four sidebars appear throughout the book:

MAN UP
How to bring your "A" game.

MAN DOWN
Learning from past grooms' mistakes.

CHA-CHING
Quick money-saving tips.

TRADITION SAYS
Traditional or etiquette-related facts and tidbits.

Last, you'll find a few appendixes at the back of the book designed to be quick references that you can refer to either during or after reading the book. There, you'll find a glossary and an assortment of checklists as well as additional resources to check out. This information is valuable if you want to brush up on a topic without having to re-read an entire chapter.

In closing, there's a reason why the title of this book is called "Be the Man." Contrary to how that phrase may sound to some, it represents much more than just being macho. We all already know that you're "the man" in your everyday life. Now, it's time to become "the married man." This is all about stepping up and taking an active role in preparing for the most important day of your life. Sure, it may sound funny saying that out loud or admitting to your friends that you're gung-ho about planning your wedding. But I guarantee that you'll garner more respect than embarrassment for being a hands-on groom.

Take it from a graduate of groom school: your wedding day will be over in a flash. Do you really want to look back on the day and wish you had been more involved? I know a lot of guys whose wedding-planning involvement consisted of nothing more than showing up to pose for photos and saying "I do." When those guys hear about some of the great things going on in the world of grooms today, they get a little jealous (and rightfully so).

Above all, I hope that this book gets you excited, inspires you, and disproves the age-old myth that wedding planning is only for brides.

Cheers!

Acknowledgments

Some guys love taking all the credit for an achievement. I am not one of them. There are many people without whom this book would not have been possible.

To my good friend, Mr. Johnnie Walker: your companionship kept me motivated throughout the writing process and helped inspire ideas when I would hit that proverbial "brick wall."

To my fellow wedding industry colleagues and bloggers: thank you for your support and for consistently creating fantastic content that not only inspires brides and grooms but also me.

To my wife and family: your support means the world to me. Wherever life takes you, you can count on me to be right beside you, cheering you on. I'm your biggest fan.

To The Man Registry® Team: I'm extremely proud of what we've created and the often painstaking steps we've taken to get here. This book represents a huge step for The Man Registry®, and I'm pumped to see where we go next.

To my writing partner, Kara Horner, who co-wrote this book with me: Where to begin? I'm proud to call you a partner and honored to call you a friend. Thank you for taking on such an intense workload and having the patience to put up with my grammar errors, choppy sentences, and bad jokes. Trust me, I know it wasn't easy. This book wouldn't have been possible without you, and I'm immensely grateful for your contributions. Thank you!

Engagement Ring Shopping

Before you can become the groom, you first have to lasso in a bride. And before you can do that, you have to show her that you're the only guy in the world ever worth saying "yes" to. Now, I'm not talking about giving her endless love, affection, and trust. That stuff is easy compared to your first mission: buying the perfect engagement ring. Statistics tell us that 86 percent of women only get engaged for the ring. And personally, I think that number is a little low. After I proposed to my wife, I think she spent more time looking at her new finger candy than at me.

In all seriousness, there is no magic formula for finding the ring of her dreams. But if you do your homework, the process becomes much simpler. Remember, as corny as it sounds, the focus should be on what the ring symbolizes, not how many carats it has.

How Much Should You Spend?

You've probably been wondering how much coin you should be prepared to drop on an engagement ring. You're not alone. At the top of the list of most-asked questions in the history of mankind, "How much should I spend on the ring?" is a close second to "Which came first: the chicken or the egg?"

Setting your bling budget is the first (of many) important decisions you'll make throughout the wedding-planning process. But remember, this isn't the time for hasty decisions or impulse buys. Try thinking of this ring as a pair of World Series tickets. If you had one chance to pick any seat available, you'd pick the best one you could afford, right? Your decision may mean staying in one night per weekend for the next six months or buying a 42-inch TV instead of the 60-inch version, but it'll be worth it.

TRADITION SAYS
Before you commit to spending the commonly expected two-month's salary on her engagement ring, remember that traditions aren't set in stone. Use this dollar amount as a starting point for the conversation, but remember the big picture: what you're comfortable spending.

You've probably been exposed to the popular school of thought that you should spend two months of your salary on the engagement ring. This is a common rule of thumb to consider when determining your budget, but it's by no means a mark to which you should feel tied. Let's face it: some guys have a lot more disposable income than others. Spending $2,500 on a ring doesn't make you any less of a man than dropping $8,000. In fact, I'd argue that it makes you a lot smarter because you're being realistic about your budget. The average engagement ring purchase in 2010 was $5,300.

I strongly encourage you to talk to friends who have been through this process before. If they're comfortable telling you what they spent, you'll start to get an idea of how much bang you'll get for your buck. It's also very wise to be honest with your jeweler about your budget. He or she will be able to walk you through a series of options to fit your gal's desires.

Finding Out What She Likes

If it were as simple as just buying the first ring you see, you probably wouldn't be reading this chapter. It's important to start the engagement the right way by giving her the ring of her dreams. This involves doing some research and even getting her involved. With so many options available, you don't want to make a completely uneducated guess and risk disappointing her.

Even if you're planning a surprise proposal, taking her ring shopping is a great idea. Most likely, at this point in your relationship, you both know that marriage is on the horizon—so why not see what ring options are out there ahead of time and get a better idea of what she likes? Remember, this is a ring that she'll wear every day and should absolutely love. Although you don't have to tell her how much you're planning to spend or whether you'll absolutely be buying a specific ring, at least you'll have her input—which will make this big purchase easier when the time comes. She'll definitely appreciate the opportunity to clue you in on what she has in mind.

 MAN UP
Not 100 percent sure what type of ring she's expecting? Bring along her best friend while you're ring shopping so you can really impress your girlfriend with a choice that fits her tastes.

If you're totally against her knowing the proposal is on the way, your next best resource is enlisting her friends and family to help. Surely at some point, she has dropped hints to them on what her ideal ring might look like. Try picking her best girlfriend's brain for hints. She should be happy to help. If not, tell her she's out of the wedding party and see whether that helps change her mind (I kid!).

Types of Rings

Engagement ring styles range from Amy Adams to Zooey Deschanel to Kim Kardashian. In other words, some are elegantly simple, some have unique style, and others are flashy and elaborately designed. After you've gotten the gist of what she's looking for, it's time to do some research of your own on the various types of rings.

Diamonds

In case you haven't watched TV or been to a mall in the last 20 years, diamonds are by far the most popular stone for engagement rings and jewelry in general. With so much conflicting information on diamonds, however, it's best to focus on the four areas that everyone agrees on: the "four Cs." Made up of clarity, color, cut, and carat, these areas help determine the value of the diamond.

 MAN UP
You'll be a step ahead of the rest if you walk into the jewelry store with an understanding of the four Cs and other common jewelry terminology. This will tell the jeweler that you mean business, and the process will go that much smoother.

Clarity is determined by the number, size, nature, and location of any internal inclusions and external blemishes (the number of crystals or clouds that can be seen using 10X magnification). In regular guy's terms, clarity is the clearness and purity of a diamond. Now, before you start worrying about being able to afford a flawless diamond, remember that 99 percent of the time your fiancée will be looking at her ring with a naked eye. Unless she has superhuman vision, there really won't be a noticeable difference. A medium-clarity diamond is just as striking as a flawless one.

Color is the amount of color that a diamond contains. The majority of diamonds have a hint of yellow or brown, but a perfect diamond is perfectly transparent with no hue. Keep in mind that the vast majority of diamonds are not perfect.

Cut refers to the proportions, finish, symmetry, and polish of the diamond. Technically speaking, a diamond's cut doesn't actually refer to its shape but rather its reflective qualities. A diamond's angles and finish are what determine its capability to handle light, which creates the sparkling effect that girls love.

The last, but not least, of the four Cs is carat. Carats are the unit of weight by which diamonds are measured, meaning that the larger the diamond, the higher the carat. Because larger diamonds are rare, they're more valuable. Two half-carat diamonds put together won't cost as much as a single one-carat diamond because the one-carat diamond is rarer.

So why stop at four? Certificates are sometimes referred to as the "fifth" C. A diamond certificate, or grading report, is a certified evaluation of your diamond that includes grades for all four Cs. To be valid, the grades must be given by a qualified professional. No matter where you buy your diamond, insist on receiving a copy of the certification.

In addition to the "four Cs," it would also be wise to study up on the various diamond cuts and the positives and negatives of each. There are multiple options to choose from, so be sure to discuss preferences with her before getting your heart set on one. Here are some of the more popular cuts:

- **Round cut:** This is the most popular of the diamond cuts. If you're the paranoid type, you'll be happy to know that this cut is held in by six prongs for increased stability. This bling isn't going anywhere.

- **Princess cut:** This cut features a square top that's designed to showcase color. Because this setting is only held in by four prongs, be aware that it's more likely than the round cut to come loose.

- **Oval cut:** If she's a fan of the round cut but wants something a tad different, an oval cut diamond might do the trick. While not as popular as round, this unique cut will certainly stand out.

- **Pear shaped diamonds:** This cut is gaining in popularity and is another stand-out cut. If you're considering this option, check with your jeweler to make sure they're comfortable working with this style, as it's not as common as other cuts.

Cubic Zirconia

All joking aside, cubic zirconia (or CZ) is more common than you probably think. While sometimes thought of as nothing more than a wanna-be diamond, this synthetic rock can actually be a valid alternative option for guys who are not yet able to purchase the diamond of her dreams. You and your bride may decide that instead of dropping mucho bucks at Tiffany's, you'd rather commit those dollars to the honeymoon or a down payment on a house. In my humble opinion, it's really not a bad move. If you both agree on cubic zirconia, go for it with the mindset that this is merely a temporary placeholder for that bigger, better ring to come in the future.

Because of the stigma often associated with cubic zirconia, this option can be risky. If you don't include her in the process and end up buying CZ, you may be signing a one-way ticket to the doghouse. This topic needs to be discussed as a team.

Other Stones

After all that has been drilled into your head about diamonds being a girl's best friend, is there any way you can possibly give her an engagement ring that doesn't include a diamond? Without question, the answer is yes.

Tanzanite (a brown gemstone), sapphire (a blue gemstone), emerald (a green gemstone), and ruby (a red gemstone) are four of the most popular non-diamond engagement rings on the market. While not for everyone, these non-diamond engagement rings bring something new to the table if you and your girl feel like you're drowning in diamonds. As always, I strongly recommend sitting down and spending some time talking with your fiancée-to-be about what ring styles she likes. She will, after all, be the one wearing the ring.

Eco-Friendly Options

Who doesn't want a clean Earth? If you're an environmentally friendly couple, you may want to do research on eco-friendly diamonds and jewelry before getting too far into the shopping process. Unfortunately, not all engagement rings are created equally. I'm sure you've heard the term *blood diamond* or seen the movie of the same name. Unfortunately, there are many diamond-mining methods that lead to violence and human rights abuses as well as damage to the environment.

Here are a few green buzzwords to keep in mind as you and your bride-to-be search for the ideal ring that looks great and also makes you feel good about yourselves:

- Made from recycled or renewed metals and materials
- Uses FairTrade gold
- Comes from conflict-free sources
- Promotes fair labor and sustainable practices
- Lab-created or synthetically grown diamonds

The Ring's Band

Just when you think you're done making decisions, the jeweler is inevitably going to ask you what type of band and setting you want. While not as big of a game-changer as the stone, these choices can be confusing if you're not prepared. Again, get her input beforehand on what her ideal ring looks like. Consider the width and thickness of the band, her ring size, and her skin tone. Also, take a peek at her current jewelry collection and see whether there is an overwhelming amount of one type of metal. Silver, gold, and white gold all make fantastic choices. However, if you're looking for durability, go with platinum.

When determining the setting of the stone, be careful not to go overboard. Some guys will request that the stone be set up high to show it off. However, that can be seen as gaudy in many circles and also make it more prone to snagging. It can also make the ring uncomfortable for your fiancée. Imagine wearing a ring on *your* finger that sticks up three inches, and I think you'll understand. I recommend a subtle setting. This way, you're being modest and classy at the same time.

Ways to Save Money

When buying a ring, you'll want to get the most for your money. Diamond and stone prices vary from store to store because no two pieces are exactly alike. It may be time consuming, but it pays to do your research and shop around. Go to several larger chain stores and price what you want. We then suggest checking out a few smaller mom-and-pop stores or a preferred jeweler that your family has used in the past. Pay them a visit and compare prices. You never know where you could find your diamond in the rough.

$ **CHA-CHING**
Are you planning on giving her a completely custom engagement ring? If you're crafty and have experience working with jewelry, you can create a design yourself as opposed to paying a jeweler to do so.

You can also consider financing the ring through your jeweler or credit card; however, you'll want to be careful and cover your bases. Financing can be great because it enables you to pay for the large purchase in chunks, but you don't want to end up flushing too much money away in interest payments. My advice is to pay for the cost of the entire ring at once if you can afford it. This way, you aren't signing your soul away with so many big expenses on the horizon during your engagement.

Another way to save money is not buying a new ring at all. If there's a treasured family heirloom ring that belonged to her mother, grandmother, or other family member, it might make the engagement significantly more meaningful to your fiancée. This route isn't for everyone, so make sure you're fully confident that this is something she'll appreciate. In most cases, you can even have an individual stone placed on a new setting (or vice-versa). A true win-win situation, going this route not only saves money but also adds sentimental value.

Determining Her Ring Size

After you've decided on a ring, the next step is telling the jeweler what size the ring should be. Trust me: this is one area where size *does* matter. When you pop the question and present her with the ring, you don't want it to slide right off her finger. If you're planning a stealth proposal, here are my top six ways to determine her ring size without blowing the surprise.

- Get in touch with a family member or friend of your lady. If they've ever bought her a ring before, they'll know her ring size. You could even recruit someone to take her shopping "for fun" to try on some rings.

- If there's a ring that she wears on her left ring finger, discreetly swipe it from her jewelry drawer for a day and take it to your jeweler to determine the size. If you can't get it out of the house, be resourceful and make a mold of the ring in a bar of soap. You can do this by simply wetting down a bar of soap until it's moist enough to push one of her old rings into it, forming a mold of the size of the ring. Remove the ring and let the soap harden back up. Then take the bar to your jeweler and they'll easily be able to determine the size.

- While she's sleeping, wrap a piece of string around her ring finger and mark the size. Any jeweler will be able to translate this into her ring size. While you're at it, leave her hand soaking in a bowl of warm water. You may not be able to pull pranks like these after you get married, so get them in while you still can. (Just kidding!)

- Test her trust by telling her that you're purchasing a ring for someone else. If your mom or sister has an upcoming birthday, this plan might actually work.

- Do some research on ring sizing and make an educated guess. Remember to err on the side of caution. Rings can be sized down much more easily than they can be sized up.

- Just ask her. If you've been together long enough, she probably assumes that you'll be popping the question eventually. You don't have to tell her when and where it will be. Just let her know that you're putting the information on file.

MAN DOWN
Don't assume that her right-hand ring finger is the same size as her left. Believe it or not, the size of fingers can vary from hand to hand.

Ring Insurance

Now that you've found the ring that perfectly shows how much you love your bride-to-be (or as much as a rock can tell her), don't forget that final, all-important step in the ring-buying process: insurance. Just like all major purchases, it's extremely important to have insurance lined up before you finalize the deal. This way, when she flushes the ring down the toilet after you forget to mow the lawn, it's not a total loss.

MAN UP
When searching for jewelry insurance online, be sure to read as many reviews as you can find. Reviews will help lead you toward a reputable company that you won't regret using.

A variety of companies specialize in insuring your valuable jewelry. A simple Internet search is one way to find these companies. However, your best bet is to ask the jeweler for recommendations before you make your purchase. Often, they have a preferred insurer with whom they routinely work. Some of the larger jewelry chains may even have an in-house insurance department (which will make your life a lot easier). You can also research the possibility of adding the ring to your homeowner's or renter's insurance policy.

Whichever insurance route you choose, you'll need to have a valid appraisal of the ring that declares the piece's worth. Without this, the insurance company would have no idea what to charge you to protect it. Your jeweler should offer an appraisal as part of the purchase. If they don't, ask for one. After you've finalized the insurance arrangement, keep the appraisal in a safe place, such as a safety deposit box or in a hidden underground bunker.

If this is your first go-round in insuring jewelry, here are a few questions to answer before signing your name on the dotted line:

- Does the policy only cover accidental damage and theft? Are there any scenarios in which the ring isn't covered?

- How do you go about filing a claim, and how does the insurance handle replacing the damaged or lost ring?

- How would you be compensated for a one-of-a-kind or rare stone that's not readily available?

The pressure to score the perfect engagement ring can easily send a guy running for the hills. Don't do it. Remember, you're not living in a jewelry commercial. The best thing you can do is familiarize yourself with the steps and information in this chapter and make the decision that's best for you, your bank account, and your soon-to-be bride.

The Rules of Engagement

So you're ready to take one of the biggest steps in a man's life and pop the question. Congrats! This is a huge milestone—one you'll both remember for the rest of your lives. So it definitely pays to put some serious thought into it beforehand.

Telling the Family

Before you devise the perfect way to propose, take a cue from past generations and ask her family for permission. Traditionally, the groom-to-be asked his future father-in-law for permission to marry his daughter. While some guys might think this tradition is antiquated and no longer necessary in modern times, I beg to differ. Simply asking your girlfriend's father—as well as her mother (or whomever raised her, such as grandparents or an aunt)—for their blessing and informing them of your intent to marry their daughter is a respectful gesture that will not only score points with your future in-laws but also with your bride-to-be—especially if she has a close relationship with her folks.

One exception: if she has a strained or non-existent relationship with one or both parents, you can skip seeking out his or her permission. There's no need to push things in this case.

On the flip side, if you find yourself in a much more tense situation and already expect that her dad or parents may not readily give you their blessing to marry their daughter for whatever reason (be strong, man), consider asking for permission anyway. Even if they say no, at least you'll have informed them of your intentions and possibly scored some points with your bride-to-be by reaching out to them.

MAN DOWN
Although tradition suggests that you only need to ask your girlfriend's father for permission to marry her, don't forget to ask her mother as well. After all, she also helped raise her daughter to become the amazing woman she is today.

What's the best way to ask them? Face-to-face is always preferable. While it's probably easiest to talk to both parents at the same time, feel free to ask them separately if it seems less intimidating. For example, if her dad's into fishing, ask him out for a day on the lake to broach the subject, and then let her mom in on the good news when you get back. But if you're planning to talk to both parents together, ask them to dinner (or, at a minimum, invite yourself over for a chat).

If her parents live out of state or in another country, you're sure to score some extra points by making an effort to either drive or hop a flight to chat with them in person. However, if traveling just isn't possible, a phone call (acceptable) or Skype session (even better) will suffice. Otherwise, try to make every effort to meet with them in person. This is an important occasion for them, too.

Are you nervous? Don't be. Your girlfriend's parents will most likely be overjoyed at the news and will truly appreciate your sincere effort to let them in on your plans.

Proposing

Believe it or not, the way you pop the question is a big deal. Your proposal will not only make an impression on your future fiancée but on your friends and family as well. Don't let that scare you. The key is to put some serious thought into the proposal and make it as personal and original as possible.

This is no time to rush into anything. The goal is to really wow her and make her feel special. The most impressive proposals require taking the time to devise the perfect plan.

That said, if your girlfriend hates any and all public displays of affection and definitely wouldn't be into a flashy proposal made in front of others, it's probably wise to respect that and go low-key. But just because you're keeping it on the down-low doesn't mean you can't make it special for the two of you. At least consider what you'll say ahead of time to make it extra meaningful.

Proposal Tips

First, make sure to add some bling. There really should be no excuses here. Even if times are tough and you're short on cash, it's important to propose with some type of ring, whether it's a diamond sparkler, a family heirloom, or a temporary placeholder (for ring shopping tips, see Chapter 1). Proposing with a ring shows her that you're serious about marriage and that this isn't a decision you've taken lightly.

When it comes to deciding what you'll say to her, it might help to write down a few things beforehand so your mind doesn't go blank in the heat of the moment. Although it may sound obvious, the best advice is to speak from your heart. Jot down some of the reasons why you love her, why she's special, and why you want to spend the rest of your life with her. There's no need to agonize over the perfect wording here.

MAN UP
Make sure to get down on one knee when you propose. Some may say that chivalry's dead, but this definitely isn't the occasion to test that theory. Score points with your future fiancée as well as her friends and family by staying true to tradition.

What should you do if your nerves kick in? It may sound simple, but try taking a few deep breaths before you go for it. You'll feel more relaxed if you slow down a bit. If you're worried about botching your speech, try practicing your delivery in front of a mirror beforehand. And if all else fails, have a drink before taking the plunge. A little liquid courage might just do the trick to ease your nerves.

Once you've devised your game plan, don't forget to get down on one knee as you pop the question. This is another important step that will really impress her, her family, and her friends as well as solidify your status as a true gentleman. Besides, if you don't, you'll never live it down. (Trust me—I've heard the horror stories.)

However you decide to propose, stay cool and confident. After all, your girlfriend wouldn't have put up with you for this long if she didn't think you were "the one." It's time to wife up. You've got this, man.

Creative Proposal Ideas

Once you're ready to craft your proposal concept, start by thinking about activities that are meaningful to your girlfriend or your relationship. Try answering a few questions to get your creativity flowing. For example, if she had a free day to focus on herself, how would she spend it? What did you do on your first date? What do you both love doing together in your free time?

While there's nothing wrong with a basic dinner date, take some inspiration from truly creative grooms and think outside the (ring) box. Here are a few proposal concepts from other grooms to help spark some ideas:

- If she loves being pampered but never takes time for herself, treat her to a spa day, complete with a massage, facial, and manicure/pedicure. Have a car pick her up and deliver her there so that it's a true surprise. Follow it up with a romantic dinner where you'll pop the question.

- Does she love shopping? Take her shopping for a new dress or outfit to wear on your special evening. For extra points, throw in new shoes or jewelry. Seal the deal by proposing in a scenic or historic location nearby.

- Is she outdoorsy? Arrange a hike or a bike ride through a serene forest or national park, and arrange a surprise picnic at the end—complete with champagne for celebrating après-proposal.

- Is she a die-hard sports fan? (Seriously, don't let her get away!) Take her to see her favorite team play a big game at home or in a cool away-game destination. Skip the Jumbotron proposal—it's overdone, and she might expect it.

- Does she love adventure? Treat her to a helicopter or hot-air balloon ride above your city or a place she's been dying to visit, then finish it off with an amazing dinner. Pop the question while you're in the air, if it seems like the right time (just make sure there's no chance of dropping the ring!), or during dinner afterward.

- Does she love trying new things? Treat her to a couples' cooking class, a vineyard tour, or a wine tasting. Make sure the instructor or tour guide is in on your plans and can aid in the process when needed.

- Is she the sentimental type? Recreate your first date or another important relationship milestone. Include as many special touches as possible to really impress her with your attention to detail.

Remember, your engagement is a story that you'll both tell for years to come, so go the extra mile and make it truly memorable.

Including Family and Friends

Another way to make the engagement special is to involve your girl-friend's family and closest friends (as well as yours), either by enlisting them to help with the surprise plans or by inviting them to celebrate with you afterward. She'll never forget being able to share this important occasion with them, and they'll truly appreciate your gesture to include them.

MAN UP
Need someone to help document the occasion? Enlist one of her siblings or friends to videotape or photograph the proposal from afar so that you'll always have this special day—and her reaction—on record.

Does she have a sister who lives out of state? Fly her in to celebrate with you after the proposal. You'll earn extra points with both ladies, and your fiancée will always remember that her sister was there to share in this special moment.

What *Not* to Do

Whatever you do, don't make these deal-breaking mistakes during your proposal:

- Say anything that resembles the infamous "Sh*t or Get Off the Pot" proposal from the movie *The Bachelor*

- Tell her she's so smokin' hot that you know she'll never get fat

- Ramble on about how great her mother looks and that it's a sign that your girlfriend will look just as great when she's an old lady

- Say that you love the fact that she's a stellar cook and house cleaner

- Mention that you're doing this to get your grandmother off your back

- Use the words "child-bearing hips" or "amazing rack," unless your girlfriend likes hearing those things (and if so, seriously, what are you waiting for?)

Engagement Parties

Once you've let your friends and family in on the big news, they may offer to throw an engagement party to celebrate your impending nuptials. These parties are typically held within three months of your engagement and are a great excuse to gather your peeps together to eat, drink, and be merry prior to the wedding.

According to tradition, the bride's family should have the opportunity to throw the first engagement party. However, today, the groom's family, both families, friends, or other relatives of the couple may offer to throw these parties as well. Engagement parties are often held at the host's home or at a restaurant and can range from something as simple as a casual backyard cookout or cocktail party to a formal, multi-course, sit-down dinner.

Who's invited? Typically, family and close friends of the couple make up the guest list. This occasion is often the first opportunity for extended family of the couple to meet and may even be the first time that the couple's parents meet each other.

Keep in mind that the people you invite to the engagement party should also be included on your wedding guest list. An exception: if you're planning a destination wedding and a limited number of guests will be able to attend, you might want to invite those who can't make it to the wedding to your engagement party instead.

MAN DOWN
Don't invite someone to the engagement party if they won't also be invited to the wedding. They'll wonder what happened later on if they don't receive a wedding invitation, and you'll risk hurting their feelings.

Think toasts are reserved for the wedding? Think again. Toasts are often given at the engagement party as well. Traditionally, the father of the bride-to-be gives the first toast, followed by the groom-to-be, and then anyone else who'd like to wish the couple well.

Make sure to have a few words prepared ahead of time for your toast. Key points to include are toasting your bride-to-be, her family, and yours. It's also nice to thank everyone in attendance and tell them you're looking forward to celebrating with them on the wedding day.

Although gifts aren't required at engagement parties, guests may bring small gifts for the couple. It might be helpful to start registering for a few things before the invitations are sent out, just in case.

Can you skip the engagement party? Absolutely; it's not a requirement. While some couples may have one or more engagement parties, others may not have any at all. But if someone offers to throw one for you, you should accept their kind gesture. While you might feel that it's unnecessary, declining could hurt their feelings and make you seem ungrateful. However, if you're planning on a short engagement and the wedding will be held within six months, holding an engagement party so close to the wedding date might seem inappropriate.

Picking a Date

Choosing your wedding date is typically the first step that you and your fiancée will take to get the ball rolling on your wedding plans. Most often, this date is based on nailing down available openings for both your ceremony and reception sites.

While weekends, especially Saturdays, are the most popular dates for holding weddings, some couples choose to get married on a weekday to reduce costs or to book a popular venue that has a long waiting list (holding your reception in the afternoon instead of the evening may also help reduce costs). And because of their favorable weather, spring, summer, and fall are the most common wedding seasons, although weddings are held year-round.

MAN UP
Consider sending "Save the Date" cards, which are a great way to give your guests a heads up about your upcoming wedding date, especially if you plan to hold it over a holiday weekend or around a time of year when many people travel (spring break, summer, Christmas, and so on).

For some couples, choosing to hold their wedding over a holiday weekend, such as Thanksgiving, New Year's, Memorial Day, Independence Day, or Labor Day, may mean that guests coming in from out of town can stay for an extra day of celebration without having to take time off work. However, keep in mind that some of your guests may have other traditional holiday plans that could prevent them from attending your wedding.

If you're a huge sports fan, there will likely be a few dates you'll want to avoid, if at all possible:

- The Super Bowl—held in early February

- The Final Four—held in early April (throw in March as well, if you love the March Madness leading up to the Final Four)

- The NBA and Stanley Cup Finals—held in June
- The World Series—both the playoffs and the World Series in October

Although these events would never prevent *you* from selecting a date for your wedding, per se, they may be a factor for some of the guests attending your wedding … and no one wants that. Alas, if you get some major resistance from your fiancée, don't push it too hard. Your wedding is one day and should be held sacred. Besides, you don't want to start your engagement in the doghouse.

Considering a destination wedding? Regardless of the date you choose for the ceremony, it's helpful to arrange several days of activities for your guests to partake in before and after the event. This may entice more people to attend your wedding if they know you'll be there for an extended period of time and will give them more to do.

After you've popped the question and are officially engaged, sit back and enjoy it a bit before rushing right into your wedding plans (this advice goes for your fiancée as well). You most likely have plenty of time to plan, and you don't want to feel burned out or overwhelmed right out of the gate. Take a little time to relax and let it all sink in a bit, celebrate with friends and family, and then start tackling that wedding to-do list. Cheers!

Your (Wedding Planning) Plan of Attack

Now that you've secured a bride and picked a date, it's time to get into the heavy-lifting and start planning this wedding. The average engagement lasts about a year. This may seem like an über-long time, but you'll be shocked at how fast the wedding doomsday clock ticks. After the obligatory engagement celebration, it's important to start putting together a game plan as soon as possible so you don't get caught with your pants down.

What Grooms Can Get Excited About

Getting involved in wedding planning doesn't mean you have to take a sudden interest in floral motifs or start designing inspiration boards. The wedding may be known as the "bride's big day," but you're getting married, too, right? Because the wedding is a celebration of both of your lives, there's plenty of room to incorporate your tastes and interests into the overall theme. After I got engaged, I dove head first into planning because I didn't want to look back on the biggest day of my life and regret not having my input included. I planned the rehearsal dinner at my favorite brewery, catered by my favorite barbecue joint. I also incorporated my love for the St. Louis Cardinals into my groom's cake.

The opportunities to customize aspects of the wedding to your liking will be plentiful. I urge you to take advantage of them.

Every groom is different, however. How much of your own personal flavor you'd like to add to your wedding is entirely up to you.

If you're feeling a bit overwhelmed or aren't sure where to start, here are a few ideas to help get your creative juices flowing:

- Music is a huge part of the wedding day. If you're musically inclined, try writing a custom song for the ceremony or reception. And if you're feeling really courageous, consider performing it yourself.

- If you enjoy working with your hands, it's not out of the question to design and craft your own wedding rings.

- Are you a culinary genius? Try creating a new dish or perfecting an old family favorite to be served at the rehearsal dinner or wedding reception.

- There's always room to incorporate sports. From the groomsmen's attire to cakes to venues, don't be afraid to show your team spirit on the big day.

- If you're an artist or graphic designer, there's no shortage of design work for a wedding. Save-the-date cards, invitations, and programs are great outlets to showcase your skills.

MAN UP
Want to share your wedding triumphs on the Internet? Groom
bloggers are becoming a major force in the wedding blogosphere
by sharing their planning experiences and pitfalls with the world.
A blog or wedding website is also a great outlet to gain feedback
and insight on your ideas.

The Groom's Traditional Duties

Every couple will have different ways of dividing up the wedding budget
and tasks. However, these are the items that the groom is traditionally
tasked with covering:

- Wedding day transportation
- Bride's bouquet
- Marriage license
- Clergy fee
- Writing vows (if appropriate)
- Arranging and booking the honeymoon
- The bride's wedding band
- The bride's gift
- Groomsmen, usher, and ring bearer gifts
- Groom's wedding day attire
- Rehearsal dinner

Budgeting

Vacations and new home purchases aren't the only things that a bumpy economy can take a toll on. Tough financial times have caused many couples to get more creative with smaller budgets. This has led to fewer blowout weddings and more do-it-yourself planning. Yet, this isn't necessarily a bad thing. Contrary to what you may have heard, bigger isn't always better.

No matter how big or small of a wedding you want, it's extremely important to develop a budget up front and stick to it.

Determining Your Budget

How much does a wedding cost? While there's no definite answer (not all weddings are created equal), the average cost of a wedding in 2010 was just less than $28,000. However, that figure doesn't include the honeymoon, so you'll need to have additional funds set aside for your post-wedding vacation. (Find more on this topic in Chapter 12.)

Before the first dollar is spent, take a look at your personal finances as a couple. Evaluate areas where you can make cuts, and eliminate discretionary spending. The following chart illustrates the budget breakdown of an average wedding as of 2010.

CHA-CHING
It's better to be safe than sorry. When you settle on your final budget, remember to add 15 percent to account for unexpected costs and up-charges. And if you don't use that 15 percent, don't worry. You'll already have spending money set aside for the honeymoon.

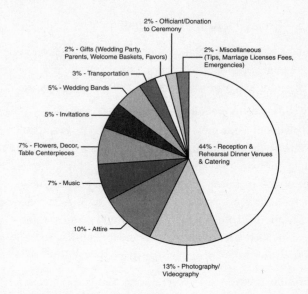

2% - Officiant/Donation
to Ceremony

2% - Gifts (Wedding Party,
Parents, Welcome Baskets, Favors)

2% - Miscellaneous
(Tips, Marriage Licenses Fees,
Emergencies)

3% - Transportation

5% - Wedding Bands

5% - Invitations

7% - Flowers, Decor,
Table Centerpieces

7% - Music

10% - Attire

44% - Reception &
Rehearsal Dinner Venues
& Catering

13% - Photography/
Videography

*Does NOT include engagement ring or honeymoon

Wedding spending broken down.

Who Pays for What?

The bride's family has traditionally covered the bulk of the wedding costs, while the groom's major contribution has been the rehearsal dinner and honeymoon. However, this tradition has changed over the years. With couples getting married at increasingly older ages, brides and grooms are now footing more of the wedding bill on their own.

It's important to have a discussion with both families to determine how much each side is willing to contribute to the wedding. Never make assumptions about these contributions until you've had that conversation. Once you know how much you'll be receiving from your family and hers, apply it to your overall budget to see what you and your fiancée will be on the hook for.

Tips for Staying on Budget

With so many expenses, it can be tough to keep yourself on budget. If you find yourself going overboard, don't freak out. Remind yourself that wedding planning is a process; therefore, there will be ups and downs.

If things are starting to get out of control, take a step back and re-evaluate. There are plenty of areas in which you can cut back, even if you're already in the midst of planning. The guest list is a natural place to start. Purchasing your own food and liquor (or eliminating liquor entirely), using your own transportation, skipping a DJ or band in lieu of an iPod, or using friends as vendors also provide opportunities to reduce costs. Additionally, many vendors will offer discounts if you're referred by a past client. Your married friends are another great resource, so be sure to ask them whether they know of any budget-friendly vendors.

On the flip side, there are also several ways that you can gain a return on your spending. Putting money into a high-yield money market or CD account for several months prior to the wedding can earn you some extra bucks that you otherwise wouldn't have. There are also a plethora of credit cards that offer rewards based on certain types of spending. For example, finding a card that offers generous airline mile rewards might be perfect for a groom who's concerned about the honeymoon budget or is planning a destination wedding. A quick online search can provide a wealth of credit card options. Just be sure to never charge more than you can afford. As you surely know, a credit card isn't a free pass to unlimited spending.

Finally, I advise against taking out a loan for your wedding spending. Newlyweds face enough financial challenges when starting out, even without having new debt to take on. Wouldn't you rather put your money toward building your man cave than paying down loan interest?

Creating a Timeline and Sticking to It

Let's face it: you have a busy life. Between friends, family, and your fiancée, there's hardly enough time for your hobbies, let alone time for planning a wedding. The more organized you can be, the smoother the process will go. If you're an over-achiever, you might consider turning your office or a spare bedroom into a wedding "war room," complete with dry-erase boards, checklists, and a budget-tracker.

Setting goals and conquering checkpoints is key to staying on pace. Here's a list of the major tasks you should have accomplished at strategic times during the wedding-planning process.

MAN UP
Using software programs such as Word or Excel are a great way to track your planning timeline and stay on budget. Between computers and smart phones, it's extremely easy to share this information with your fiancée in real time.

Twelve Months Before the Wedding

- Finalize the budget and wedding date.

- Find ceremony, reception, and rehearsal dinner venues.

- Determine the theme or style of your wedding.

- Secure your officiant and sign up for marriage-prep classes (if applicable).

Nine Months Before the Wedding

- Determine your guest list and wedding party.
- Register for gifts.
- Book the caterer, videographer, photographer, transportation, and entertainment.

Six Months Before the Wedding

- Send out save-the date cards (if applicable).
- Book your honeymoon travel.
- Reserve a hotel room for the wedding night.
- Reserve hotel rooms for out-of-town guests.
- If you're having a groom's cake, secure a bakery and determine the cake's design.
- Determine your attire and the attire of your wedding party.
- Finalize the rehearsal dinner menu and itinerary.

Three Months Before the Wedding

- Select and order wedding bands.
- Purchase gifts for your bride and the wedding party.
- Send out wedding and rehearsal dinner invitations.
- Write or select vows and readings (if applicable).
- Create the wedding program or secure a vendor to handle it.

Final Month Before the Wedding

- Write your toast.

- Get the marriage license.

- Ensure that the groomsmen are fitted and have ordered their attire.

- Set up grooming appointments for yourself and the groomsmen.

Of course, if you're planning with a much shorter timeline, you can throw this list out the window. Weddings planned on shorter schedules can still be great, but expect some potential challenges—such as not being able to book all of your desired vendors, a lack of available venues, and the stress of having to cram lots of planning into a few short months.

Working as a Team

The workload may seem intense, but remember, you're not alone in this. At the risk of sounding cheesy, your bride-to-be will be there to pick you up when the going gets tough (and vice-versa). Try imagining that you're participating in a season of *The Amazing Race*. The ultimate goal is to get a kick-ass wedding planned, and the trials and tribulations of planning it might just prove to be some of the best memories (and if not, at least it will all be over soon!).

Scheduling weekly or bi-weekly date nights are a great way to kick back and relieve stress while still making some planning progress. These date nights can be anything from going out for drinks or grabbing dinner at a favorite local restaurant. Don't look at these nights as full-on wedding meetings but rather an opportunity to check in on your progress, determine trouble areas, and offer help if your fiancée is struggling with a specific planning aspect. Be open to altering plans if she's not completely sold on one of your ideas.

Surviving Marriage-Prep Classes

Are you prepared to spend a Saturday or Sunday afternoon discussing and learning about marriage? You may cringe at the thought, but if you'll be married in a church, you'll most likely be required to take part in some sort of marriage-prep course. It may sound like a drag, but this shouldn't be something to dread. If you take it seriously, you may learn something new about your fiancée as well as gain some valuable insight into what life as a married man will be like.

Marital duties, planning for children, and finances are just a few of the big-ticket topics discussed during marriage prep. The courses are designed to help you answer any lingering questions or conquer any fears you may have about your impending walk down the aisle and what comes after "I do." Classes are generally led by clergy, a marriage counselor, or a married couple volunteering their time. Depending on where you're getting married, the number and location of classes will vary. As soon as you decide on a ceremony venue, be sure to check their requirements for pre-wedding courses.

Keep in mind that you'll probably be asked to share examples of personal stories and beliefs during the classes. Many men can become nervous or self-conscious about opening up in this setting. (I was one of them!) However, I quickly learned that marriage prep is a classic example of getting out as much as you put in. There's a lot to learn if you take it seriously.

Do I Have to Go to Wedding Shows?

To quote Michael Corleone in *The Godfather Part 3*, "Just when I think I'm out, they pull me back in." Sure enough, just when you think you've laid all the groundwork for a successful wedding-planning experience, your fiancée will utter two terrifying words that will suck you right back into the madness: *wedding show.*

Spending an entire Saturday or Sunday afternoon at a bridal fair is something your brain may not be able to process. Because these events occur mostly on weekends, it's likely to conflict with a sporting event or other weekend activity that sounds a lot better than being dragged to a convention center full of women to discuss flower arrangements and bridesmaid dresses. However, men's attendance at wedding shows is rising. And before you decline the invitation, it's worth considering how you can benefit from attending.

MAN DOWN
If you decide to attend a wedding show with your fiancée, take it seriously and try to act like you want to be there. Sure, it probably won't be the best day of your life, but there's nothing more annoying to a bride than a whiny groom. Try to stay positive—or you'll risk paying for it later.

A growing trend at bridal fairs is the inclusion of a "groom's corner" or "groom's lounge." These areas showcase the vendors and businesses that grooms are more likely to handle. For example, if you're thinking about leaving your wedding ceremony or reception in a vintage Rolls-Royce or classic Corvette, a transportation vendor will be there to walk you through the options and details. Likewise, it's a great opportunity to study up on attire styles, travel agencies, and groomsmen gifts.

If you decide to boldly go where few men have gone before, here are my top five things to remember before you embark on your first (and probably last) wedding show voyage:

- Go in with an open mind, and be ready to make decisions.

- Have a plan of attack, including a list of specific vendors you want to talk to.

- Grab as many freebies and samples as you can.

- Establish your budget beforehand.

- Stay hydrated, and wear comfortable shoes.

Despite being commonly referred to as a "bridal" show, you might be surprised at what you'll learn. Worst-case scenario: pack a flask and get ready for some intense people-watching.

Dealing with Bridezilla

As much as I hope this chapter has adequately prepared you for your voyage into the world of wedding planning, I should warn you that most women look at the wedding-planning process a little differently than men do. In the months before your wedding, you may begin to notice your fiancée becoming frustrated over what you perceive to be "minor" details. Trust me, to most brides, there are no "minor" details when it comes to the wedding. This frustration may turn into a fiery rage directed at renegade wedding vendors, uncooperative bridesmaids, pushy moms, or even you! During these tough and trying times, it's important not to panic, break down, or completely call off the wedding. Believe it or not, there are ways to stop "bridezilla" in her tracks that don't involve having her committed.

Imagine that your favorite sports team has just made the World Series or Super Bowl for the first time in your lifetime. You'd be pretty ecstatic, right? In a weird way, this may be how she feels about the wedding day. As cliché as it sounds, she really has been dreaming about and looking forward to this day since she was a child. Just as your inner hooligan comes out before a big game, her inner bridezilla is bound to make an appearance when the wedding planning gets tough. It's your job to tame the beast and help her navigate these murky waters. A big part of "being the man" is to act as supportive as possible and to help her remember that this is a happy time. Remind her that as stressful as things seem, everything is going to work out swell. Of course, this is easier said than done.

One of the best ways to help her alleviate pre-wedding stress is to get her mind completely off the wedding. Here are a few ways to switch things up while making her feel like the princess she is (or thinks she is).

Wine and Dine Her

If most of her days consist of a long day at work followed by a long night of wedding planning, try surprising her with a home-cooked dinner. It doesn't have to be gourmet, but a fish or a chicken entrée with vegetables on the side generally pleases most palates (bonus: fewer carbs means she won't blame you for feeling like an ogre when trying on wedding dresses).

Stage a Movie Night

The movie should absolutely *not* be wedding related and preferably not even a chick flick. Go for a classic comedy complete with popcorn, candy, and wine. Consider this a night of indulgence. The only rule is no wedding talk.

Be Her "Yes" Man

For a night or weekend, suck it up and make "yes, dear" the standard answer to everything she asks of you. I know this isn't always easy, but if you succeed, she may be the one saying yes or rewarding you later for good behavior.

If all of these options fail, there is only one other piece of advice I can offer you: run!

The Wedding Party and Guest List

What good is planning an epic wedding if your friends and family aren't there to share in the fun? One of the first tasks you'll encounter during your wedding-planning journey will be mapping out who to invite to your wedding and who to assign the honored roles of best man, groomsmen, and ushers.

I think you'll find that there's a lot of common sense that goes into making these types of decisions. That said, it's important to be organized and think everything through. You can't take back a wedding invite or a spot in the wedding party, so work with your fiancée to make sure you have all your ducks in a row before finalizing your decisions.

Assembling the Wolf Pack

Just when you think you've "popped the question" for the one and only time in your life, think again. You'll soon be popping several more questions—this time, to your wedding party members. Don't be alarmed: the preparations for these "proposals" aren't nearly as strenuous.

Your best man and groomsmen represent a collection of your closest friends and confidants. Some relationships may fade over time, but these are the guys who have been unwavering in their friendship and support over the years. To reference pop culture, think of these guys as your own personal "wolf pack."

TRADITION SAYS

Give your wedding party members a heads up about the planned wedding date and their expected duties. While it isn't necessary to begin asking them immediately after the engagement, you should lock down your best man, groomsmen, and other positions within nine months of the wedding day.

On the groom's side, wedding party members typically include brothers, close friends, relatives, and siblings of the bride. While there's no golden rule here, it's traditionally considered appropriate to include, in some capacity, people who have previously asked you to serve in their wedding party. It's also standard protocol to run your decisions by your fiancée before you ask. You should both agree on the number of attendants for each side as well as settle any potential disagreements on who should or should not be included.

And just as you planned your marriage proposal, you should try to think of creative ways to ask your boys to join the wedding party. You can make it a group event during a golf outing, a camping trip, or over dinner and drinks on the town. Or, you can opt to ask each person in private. Regardless of how you decide, it's important to convey just how much you appreciate each individual's friendship and what it would mean to have him as part of your wedding party.

Selecting Groomsmen

In medieval times, groomsmen were known as bride-knights who guarded the bride against kidnapping. While this risk hopefully won't come into play at your wedding, your groomsmen will still serve an important role. They'll be watching your back, spending mucho time with you in the lead-up to the wedding, and assisting you in various capacities on the wedding day. When rounding up your usual suspects for roles as groomsmen, think about whether they possess the following qualities:

- **They're dependable.** Groomsmen will have many responsibilities, including being fitted for attire, showing up on time to events, and being focused on their duties.

- **They're financially able to handle their role.** Being a groomsman requires monetary contributions, including taking part in planning the bachelor party, renting or buying attire, and travel/hotel costs.

- **It's logistically feasible for them to be present for the rehearsal, rehearsal dinner, and wedding day.** If the guy lives cross-country or overseas and will have trouble getting a few days off work to travel to the wedding, it may be best to just send him a simple invite instead.

- **They get along with your bride.** Your wedding shouldn't be a power struggle between a groomsman and the bride. The wedding party spends a lot of time together during the weeks leading up to the wedding. You don't want to constantly have to play the role of mediator.

- **They're people you still see yourself being close to in 10 years.** You don't want to look back on your wedding photos and ask yourself, "Who are those guys?"

MAN DOWN
Because your groomsmen will be escorting your fiancée's bridesmaids down the aisle, you need to be mindful about matching up any former flings who may not get along. Use your best judgment here. The last thing you want is bad karma—or a major scene—on your wedding day.

Selecting the Best Man

After you've settled on your groomsmen, it's time to pick the one guy you want to stand beside you as you say "I do." You probably already have a good idea of who this will be. Your best man is the guy who you've always counted on. He's the guy who has stood next to you through thick and thin. He has been your partner-in-crime. In most cases, this is your brother or best friend. However, it's not unheard of to ask your father or other adult figure to tackle this honored role.

If you happen to have multiple brothers or simply can't make the call between two great friends, don't let traditional beliefs scare you. It's certainly acceptable to have two guys share the best man duties. For my wedding, I asked each of my brothers to share in the role. It ended up being one of the best wedding decisions I made because it would have torn me up having to choose one over the other.

Best Man Duties

Contrary to popular belief, the best man has more responsibilities than simply giving a toast and planning your bachelor party. While both of those jobs are important, it's the little things he'll do for you during the wedding festivities that you'll appreciate most. I hate to break it to you, but you're going to be under a bit of stress in the weeks and days leading up to the wedding. A big part of the best man's job is to be there for you and help ease your mind by taking care of the little things so you won't have to concern yourself with them. Starting from the time you wake up or arrive to get dressed on the wedding day, he'll be by your side—keeping you focused. Depending on when the wedding takes place, you might even want to grab breakfast or play a quick nine holes beforehand. These are perfect activities for the best man to accompany you.

The best man's traditional duties are as follows:

- Organizing your bachelor party
- Accompanying you on any pre-wedding tuxedo or suit fittings
- Giving a (sober) toast to you and your bride during the rehearsal dinner or reception
- Keeping the other groomsmen and ushers in line and aware of their jobs
- Giving you a pep talk to calm any nerves before the ceremony
- Holding onto the bride's ring on the wedding day
- Signing the marriage license as a witness immediately after the ceremony
- Serving as emcee at the reception, if you don't already have a DJ or band handling that duty
- Being introduced as part of the wedding party at the reception and taking part in any group dances
- Being present and happily posing during any and all wedding day photo-ops
- Decorating and/or driving the getaway car (if applicable)
- Returning rented tuxes on the day after the wedding (if applicable)

MAN UP
Common perception is that the best man and groomsmen are all guys. However, if you have a lifelong friend who happens to be a woman, don't be afraid to ask her to serve on your side of the aisle or see whether there's a place to include her on the bride's side.

You have to get up pretty early in the morning to fool a groom. However, I do suggest keeping a close eye out for any antics or funny business on the wedding day. One of the unwritten rules of best-mandom is the duty of organizing some sort of prank. Keep your eyes open for anyone messing with your shoes or switching out your tuxedo jacket. These are common avenues that wedding pranksters will pursue. However, my money is on the best man trying to convince you he has lost the ring. My advice: don't fall for it (or protect yourself by giving him a dummy ring to hold onto instead).

Selecting Ushers

Ushers sometimes feel like an afterthought in the attendant-selection process. However, their role is extremely important and shouldn't be overlooked. Obviously, their main responsibility is seating guests as they arrive for the ceremony. A good rule of thumb to follow is having one usher per every 50 guests. However, if you have several friends or relatives who you'd like to include, usher positions are a great way to get everyone involved. Alternatively, if you're having a smaller wedding, you can always opt to have the groomsmen and best man act as ushers as well.

It's important to note that while ushers won't be standing at the altar with you, they're just as much a part of the wedding party as the best man and groomsmen. You should invite them to all the pre-wedding parties and ask them to wear the same attire as the rest of your wolf pack. It's up to you and your bride to decide whether ushers are included in wedding party photos, but my suggestion is to treat them just like your groomsmen and invite them to take part in all photo-ops. Trust me—they'll truly appreciate the gesture.

Ushers have a unique role on the wedding day. Here are five important instructions that you should give your ushers so they can successfully perform their duties:

1. Arrive at the church on time.

2. Be cordial and polite as you escort guests to their seats. Walk arm in arm with women and let male dates follow behind.

3. Be aware of seating requests and remember which side of the church the bride and groom's families are sitting.

4. Be aware of which special guests are to be seated up front or are part of the processional.

5. After the ceremony starts, ushers should sit in the back of the church and make sure that any late-arriving guests don't cause a disruption.

Making Cuts and Selecting Ancillary Positions

Let's get one thing straight right now: it's impossible to include *all* your friends and family in the wedding party. It's a tough truth to accept, because these people have been a major part of your life—and it's only natural to try to involve everyone in your wedding. Unfortunately, unless your budget and venue can accommodate a massive wedding party, you're going to have to make cuts somewhere.

After you procure the best man, groomsmen, and ushers, there are several other ancillary honors to bestow upon other friends and family members. This is an ideal time to get younger children and other relatives involved. Additionally, it's also a way to return the favor to anyone who asked you to serve in his wedding in a similar capacity.

Popular ancillary positions to divvy up with your bride are as follows:

- Ring bearer
- Junior groom or usher
- Readers
- Candle lighters
- Gift table attendant
- Guest book attendant
- Personal attendants

MAN DOWN

It's always a wise move not to disclose the names of your wedding party and ancillary selections until you've received official confirmation from each person. This way, you won't hurt someone's feelings if you originally intended him to be a groomsman but ended up bumping him down to an usher for whatever reason.

Rewarding Your Wedding Party

They've been with you every step of the way, through good times and bad. And now, they're ready to stand beside you on the day you say

"I do." Your best man, groomsmen, and ushers will be renting tuxes, planning your bachelor party, making toasts, and helping out on the big day. In other words, a simple "thanks" and a handshake isn't going to get the job done. Put some thought into what types of gifts your boys will appreciate, and consider this a down payment for the day that you serve in one of their wedding parties.

With all your other wedding costs, it's very easy to put off spending money on a set of gifts for your wedding party until the last minute. However, this can create problems if you're ordering custom items that require a longer lead time. I recommend ordering your groomsmen gifts and having them in hand at least a month before the wedding. This way, you won't have to face the wrath of your crew (and bride) when you show up empty-handed on the wedding day.

A common question among grooms is when to hand out these gifts. There's no right or wrong answer here; however, the most common and practical forum is the rehearsal dinner. This typically ensures that everyone is in the same setting and gives you an opportunity to recognize and say a few words about each guy. Other options are the bachelor party and reception; however, you do run the risk of making other guests feel left out if they're not receiving a gift.

Selecting the Perfect Gift

When selecting gifts, it's important to think about each groomsman as an individual. You wouldn't buy a beer stein for a guy who doesn't drink, right? A common pitfall that some grooms fall into is thinking that they have to buy the same item for each guy. Instead of thinking of your wolf pack as a group, think about their individual tastes and interests. The best gifts are ones they will actually use.

To help get you started, here are some popular wedding party gift categories:

- Barware and drinking accessories
- Watches
- Money clips and wallets
- Cuff links
- Pocket tools and knives
- Barbecue grilling gear
- Cigars and associated accessories
- Travel gear
- Licensed sports items featuring the logo or mascot of a favorite team

Many gifts will also include the option of being personalized or monogrammed with the recipient's name or initials. This adds an extra personal touch to the gift's presentation and sentiment. When selecting customization options, you'll likely also have the option to include text such as "best man," "groomsman," or the date of your wedding. However, I would caution against this because these gifts are intended to honor the recipients, rather than your wedding day. Your groomsmen will remember why they received the gift, so go with personalization that makes the item theirs, not yours. And be sure to get names and initials correct the first time. There are no re-dos with engraving.

MAN UP
Don't be too formal with your gifts. If you're selecting items that offer personalization or engraving, don't be afraid to use a nickname as opposed to standard initials.

How Much to Spend

How much you spend on gifts depends on your financial situation. According to market research, grooms typically spend an average of $37 on groomsmen, usher, and ring bearer gifts and an average of $54 for the best man. Based on a typical wedding party consisting of 1 best man, 4 groomsmen, 2 ushers, and 1 ring bearer, you'll be looking at shelling out around $300 for gifts. Be sure to account for this when setting your initial budget.

CHA-CHING
Are you and your fiancée planning on purchasing your attendants' gifts online? Spend some time researching websites that offer both groomsmen and bridesmaid gifts. Most websites offer free shipping on larger orders, so you'll be able to save some coin by combining the two purchases.

It's also important to remember the cash that your wedding party will be forking over in conjunction with your wedding. Between attire, gifts, putting on the bachelor party, and travel costs, they'll be racking up a decent bill in the months and days leading up to the big day. Keep this in mind as you decide on your gift budget. Wedding costs can be a strain, but the last thing you want is for your boys to feel cheated after everything's said and done.

Beyond Pocket Knives and Flasks

Shopping for men can be repetitive, especially for guys who have been in multiple weddings and received a watch at each one. If you want to go outside the box with your gift choices, you have a plethora of options. Again, it's important to think about the tastes and hobbies of your groomsmen. Here are some ideas to get the creative juices flowing.

- Put together a group outing or pre-wedding trip for you and your boys. This is a unique way to show your appreciation. Consider arranging a weekend camping trip or a private suite at the ballgame.

- Gift certificates to a favorite restaurant make a great gift, especially if they decide to take you and your new bride along with them.

- Instead of asking your groomsmen to pay for their own wedding day attire, pick up their clothing tab. This option is sure to impress if the attire consists of purchasing shirts, pants, or shoes that the guys will likely wear again in the future.

- If your budget allows, larger-ticket items such as iPods, cameras, or seats at a sporting event will surely leave a smile on any guy's face.

- Feeling extra generous? In lieu of gifts, consider a charitable donation to a cause that your group feels strongly about.

Remember, these out-of-the-box gifts often are more expensive than the standard fare. So leave room in your budget and start saving early!

The Guest List

Some of the toughest wedding-planning decisions you'll have to make pertain to the guest list. We know that the last thing you want to do is leave Great-Uncle Fred or your freshman-year roomie off the list. But, depending on your venue's capacity, you'll likely have to make cuts.

Making Your List

Because the wedding reception is typically the responsibility of the bride's family, they'll know the maximum number of guests you can invite. However, when you're preparing your initial list, disregard this number.

First, compile a list of everyone that you and your family would like to invite (if size restraints weren't an issue). Next, merge your list with the bride's family's list to see how the numbers stack up. If the combined list is below capacity, you're sitting pretty. However, chances are that you'll be over the limit. But don't freak out; it's an issue for virtually every wedding.

Unfortunately, not everyone you invite will be able to make it for the big day. One way to use this to your advantage is to consider preparing an "A" list and a "B" list. The "A" list includes the people you absolutely want to be there. The "B" list consists of everyone else. When it comes time to send out your invitations, send invites to the "A" list first. Then, when the response cards start coming in, take note of the people who won't be coming. For every person who sends regrets, send out an invitation to someone from the "B" list. Hopefully, you'll be able to get an invitation out to everyone this way.

MAN DOWN
Planning on keeping your current job for the long haul? Don't forget to include your boss on the guest list. Even if he's not your favorite person in the world, you might be helping your future career by including him. Leaving him off could result in a few awkward moments around the office later when he overhears your co-workers talking about how great your wedding was.

Whom to Invite and Whom Not to Invite

Organizing your list isn't rocket science. Your immediate family members and other relatives are no-brainers. You and your fiancée probably share an overlapping group of friends, which will help make your job easier. After the obvious choices, the shoo-ins will become less obvious. Many couples feel an obligation to invite couples whose weddings you attended.

While this is a nice gesture, it all depends on whether you're still close with the couple.

Here's an interesting scenario. You have a second cousin who lives seven states away and just had twins. You may be close, but it would take an act of God for her to make the wedding. In situations like these, it's safe to not count these people and their families toward your final head count. If possible, speak with them beforehand. They'll probably let you know they'll be sending a gift but won't be able to attend the wedding. Although they won't be making the trip, you should still send them an invitation. Many people enjoy seeing it and may also save it as a keepsake.

Co-workers can be a source of guest list controversy. It may seem natural to invite the people you spend the majority of your days with, but how many of them do you actually see outside work? I recommend only including the guys who you would see yourself still being close with if you were to leave the company. Be cautious discussing the topic of your wedding around the office. You definitely don't want to offend anyone who won't get an invite.

Are you considering inviting an ex-girlfriend you're still friends with to the wedding? Easy there, cowboy—you're treading into dangerous waters. Start by asking yourself a few questions: Am I still good friends with my ex? Does my fiancée know this person well and like her? Would it be strange or awkward if she attended your wedding? If your bride approves, there's nothing wrong with inviting her—but do it for the right reasons. This isn't the time to rub your happiness in someone's face.

Knowing Your Limits

When touring ceremony and reception venues, the first thing you'll want to get an idea of is capacity. This figure will dictate how many guests you'll be able to accommodate. It's a good rule of thumb to plan on 25 percent of your guests not being able to attend.

If you're in a capacity crunch, I recommend limiting the "and guest" invites to guests who are currently in a relationship. You'll be surprised at how much this can help. You have to remember that weddings are a great place for singles to meet. It's a pretty safe bet that your friends who are riding solo are hoping to meet some single ladies from the bride's side. It's also worth noting that a lot of your friends will see your wedding as a reunion of old friends. They may prefer not to be bogged down by bringing along a date nobody knows.

 CHA-CHING
A great way to limit the guest list is only offering plus-ones to guests who are currently in relationships. Weddings are perfect places for single friends looking to hook up anyway, right?

Disagreements

Disagreements between you and your fiancée are sure to arise when creating the guest list. I'll fill you both in on a little secret: there's no such thing as a perfect guest list. The key is to make this process a team effort and remember that if someone isn't an obvious choice to both of you, there's probably a reason.

Negotiation skills can come in handy at this point. If you really want to invite your pledge brother from college who she's not wild about, compromise by giving her the okay to invite her co-worker who you find extremely obnoxious. Of course, you can always decide together not to invite either one—just make sure it's a team decision-making effort.

Guest Accommodations

Many of your guests will be coming from out-of-town to attend your wedding. Assuming you don't want them all crashing with you, they'll need a place to stay. Most hotels offer group rates if you reserve a block of rooms in advance of your wedding. I recommend choosing two or three hotels near your venue or reception site for your guests to choose from. Because these guests will already be spending money on travel expenses, provide them with at least one budget-friendly hotel option. Generally, the hotel will impose a cut-off date by which your guests will need to reserve their room in order to qualify for the discount. So be sure to convey this to them on your wedding website or on an insert you send along with the formal invitation. The last thing you want is someone getting stuck paying full price.

In addition to providing hotel information, you should also pass along information on local attractions and restaurants that your guests can visit during their stay. These suggestions will definitely vary among age ranges. For example, it's smart to recommend a favorite karaoke bar to your college friends but not to your grandma.

One Groom's Story
Chad in Pittsburgh

As Chad and his fiancée, Rebecca, began drawing up guest list plans for their wedding, they both were aware that a major firestorm awaited them. Chad's mother and father had gone through a rough divorce several years ago, and tensions still ran very high between them. To call the situation messy would be an understatement. Rebecca was convinced that an argument would break out between the two parents at some point during the wedding day. Chad was afraid she might be right.

Unwilling to let his parents' rocky relationship stand in the way of the perfect wedding day his bride-to-be had always dreamed of, Chad decided to take matters into his own hands. He hand-wrote letters to each parent and let them know how important their involvement on the wedding day would be. He urged them both to put aside their differences for this one special day and stomach being around each other for the sake of him and his bride. The plan worked. He received phone calls from each parent within three days of sending the letters. They both told him he had nothing to worry about. Chad was even able to coax them both into having dinner with him and Rebecca three months before the wedding to discuss planning status and the wedding day itinerary. What started out as a dreadful situation actually ended up turning into a positive experience for everyone involved.

5

Registering for Gifts

Picture this scenario: your best man—the guy you spent your college years partying with, checking out girls with, and playing pick-up hoops with—hands you a set of dish towels as your wedding gift. While it's thoughtful of him to make the effort, could you help but say, "Really?"

Traditional wedding registry items are great (and also necessary) for starting your married life with your bride. Whether it's an apartment, condo, or new house, items such as bath towels, dishes, and bedding are essential requirements. But they don't necessarily stir excitement in the hearts of men. Luckily for grooms, there are certain items that guys should handle—or at least have a hand in selecting. After all, you are half of the wedding equation. I strongly encourage you to get involved with the registering process. It's the only time in your life when you'll get to create this type of wish list.

What You Have and What You Need

Before you can start the registering process, you'll need to formulate an inventory of the items you already own as well as determine whether any of your stuff might be in need of an upgrade.

If you're already living with your fiancée, this shouldn't be too hard. In these instances, you've already had a crash course on what living with each other is like. Also, you may have even already begun purchasing some items together for your home.

If you're living separately, taking this inventory might be a bit more difficult. I recommend getting together with your fiancée to go over your separate belongings about seven to nine months before the wedding day to identify any voids.

Truth be told, she probably has her eye on a few of your things that "*have* to go" anyway—and now's the perfect time to find out what those items might be. For example, your keg lamp will probably be replaced by a real, grown-up lamp. And your days of sleeping on your college bed sheets will definitely be coming to an end. These are the unfortunate casualties of the end of your bachelorhood. Just remember, you can always rent a storage locker or box up some of these things in the garage until you're ready to give them a new home in your man cave (which should be part of any man's home).

How to Register

The registering process you've been having nightmares about isn't quite the dreadful experience your fiancée's wedding magazines and TV shows would have you believe. Virtually every type of department store now offers the option of creating a gift registry. This includes sporting goods and electronics stores. The process is relatively simple. If the store you're registering in has a registry station, start there. An employee will be able to quickly get your information entered into the system. And then, the fun begins: using the scanner gun. Get your trigger finger ready, and go to town!

Additionally, through the power of the Internet, hundreds of online-only specialty registries have begun popping up over the last few years. Some of them—including TheManRegistry.com, of course—even specifically target men by featuring manly loot they can rake in on the wedding day. Other unique online registries enable you to register for sporting-event tickets, restaurant gift cards, and even steaks.

If you decide to create an online registry, do your homework. Make sure that the website is legit by searching for reviews and press. Additionally, it's a good idea to check the site's policies on shipping, returns, and taxes. Because there may not be a physical store you can walk into, their business may operate differently than a brick-and-mortar shop.

MAN DOWN
Don't include your registry information on the save-the-date cards or invitations. This is widely considered to be presumptuous and tacky (not to mention ungentlemanly). Stay classy and post this type of info on your wedding website, or let word-of-mouth spread the word instead.

Registering for Expensive Items

Some couples may balk at the idea of registering for big-ticket items such as barbecue grills, lawnmowers, or TVs. This is understandable, because the concept of a registry is to suggest specific items that your friends and family can purchase for you. However, you should never underestimate the power in numbers.

While the average amount spent on a wedding gift from a friend is $70 (and $129 from a family member), just imagine what that equates to if friends decide to team up to take down some of the big, bad items on your gift registry. In fact, it's actually common for wedding guests to go in together on larger gifts. You'll receive gifts for both the wedding and shower(s) preceding it, so don't be afraid to give your guests plenty of gift ideas, including a few larger or more expensive items. Family members such as your parents or grandparents will also most likely plan to spend more money on your gifts, so make sure they have plenty of options. After all, if you could easily afford these things on your own, you would have already bought them by now, right?

Registry Musts for Grooms

It won't be too difficult to identify the registry areas that you want to get involved with. You might not care to be involved in choosing a flatware pattern, but you probably want a say about the grilling items you register for. If mixing bowls aren't your thing, I bet there are some 3D TV floor samples to check out in the electronics section. My point is that while the registering process is a team effort, there's no harm in splitting up—even just temporarily—to scan a few items that fall under the "his" category of your wedding wish list.

Compromise is also key here. If you're comfortable giving her complete control of the bedroom and bathroom, she may turn a blind eye as you go scanner-happy in the outdoors department. Of course, I'm playing off a few stereotypes here. Obviously, every couple is different and will have a unique registry tailored to their own personal tastes. The main thing to remember is to have fun and make sure you register for a few gifts that you really want.

Not sure where to begin? Here's a guide to some groom-friendly gift categories and suggested registry items.

Tools and Home Improvement

Getting married is 99 percent positive, 1 percent negative. That 1 percent comes from the exponential growth of your "honey-do" list, which will most likely start the day after the wedding. You probably have some spare tools hanging around your place, but married life means it's time to call in the big guns. Consider registering for these essentials:

- Tool chest
- Tool set
- Stud finder
- Paintbrushes
- Ladder
- Dependable flashlight
- Lawnmower/weed whacker
- Electronic level

Barware

Drinking is the only way to make married life tolerable. (Okay, that's a joke.) But it never hurts to have a stocked bar, including all the necessary bar essentials, for occasions when you'll be entertaining guests or just relaxing at home. Consider registering for these bar must-haves and maybes:

- Kegerator
- Wine rack
- Wine chiller
- Efficient wine bottle opener

- Drink recipe book
- Drink kits (such as for mojitos, margaritas, or martinis)
- Pub table
- Bar stools
- Insulated can holders or "koozies"

MAN UP

Be aware of the return and exchange policies for all your wedding gift registries. Inevitably, you receive duplicates or items that don't turn out quite the way you'd hoped. Also ask whether the retailer offers any discounts on purchasing any remaining items you didn't receive from your registry.

Outdoor and Patio Gear

Backyards, decks, and patios are ideal spaces for entertaining guests as well as chilling with the wife on nice summer nights. You can also use your registry as a way to stock up on gear for camping and hiking trips. Consider registering for these outdoor items:

- Fire pit or chiminea
- Outdoor space heater
- Hammock
- Washers, horseshoes, or other yard games
- Lawn chairs and tables
- Cooler
- Camping equipment, such as tents, lanterns, and sleeping bags

Kitchen and Grill Gear

Foodies unite! Your wedding registry is the perfect place to collect the gear you'll need to turn your home into a culinary castle. Don't be afraid to add exotic cutlery or specialty items to your wish list. In addition to thank-you cards, you can offer invites for guests to join you at your home to sample some of your creations. Consider registering for these essentials:

- Barbecue grill
- Cedar planks
- Grilling tools
- Grill cover
- Steak knife set
- Deep fryer
- Grilling or guy-friendly cookbooks
- Meat grinder
- Specialty hot sauce or barbecue sauce

Electronics

As men, we've loved electronics ever since we got our first video game system as kids. Now that you're going to be a married man, you owe it to the rest of us to uphold the man code and turn your home into geek central. Consider registering for these tech gifts:

- Flat-screen TV
- Video game system

- Accessories (such as a mount, screen cleaner, or media storage)
- Digital camera and/or camcorder
- iPod speakers

Game Room or Den

Don't worry—getting married doesn't mean that the fun has to stop. But it might mean that your weekly poker night becomes a monthly event instead. So when it comes time to host the guys (and their gals) at your place, you'll want to be prepared. Plus, if you decide to build a man cave, you'll need to furnish it. Consider registering for these entertaining must-haves:

- Dart board
- Poker table and accessories
- Game table (such as billiards, foosball, or air hockey)
- Board games
- Pub sign or custom neon light bearing the family name

Asking for Cash

Cold, hard cash is the most common wedding gift that newlyweds receive, yet it's the hardest gift to ask for. Most consider it a faux-pas to directly ask for money. Consequently, the topic has become a wedding etiquette danger zone. Luckily for you, there are a few subtle ways you can politely get the word out that it's all about the Benjamins when it comes to your wedding. Here are three ideas.

Let both sets of parents or other close family members know that you prefer money as a wedding gift. If your family is anything like mine, word will probably spread like wildfire within a week or so.

Include a note on your wedding website. Your note should say that you prefer cash gifts because you're working to pay off student loans or save money for a new home. This is the most polite way to directly ask for money.

Start a registry through your bank. Across the country, banks are starting to offer wedding registry services that enable your guests to deposit money that will go toward the down payment on a new home (you'll find details more on alternative registries later in this chapter).

 TRADITION SAYS
When opening gifts and cards, be sure to keep a detailed list of who gave you what. Traditionally, thank-you cards are sent out within three months of your wedding. Don't be late!

If you're desperately hoping for some greenbacks, don't worry. Statistics say that close to 80 percent of your wedding guests will actually prefer to give you cash. Most have been in your shoes and realize how important money is to newlyweds who are just starting out. Older relatives in particular are more likely to give you cash. Let's face it: they're older and wiser and see greater value in money than in, say, a kegerator.

Alternative Registries

Alternative registries are like that hip, indie band that only you and a handful of your friends know about. They're new, they're quickly gaining popularity, and soon everyone will be using them. If you want to be one of the cool grooms, you'll consider creating at least one alternative registry.

By definition, an alternative registry is one that doesn't include the standard department store fare. Instead of grill tools and patio furniture, you're aiming to fund a specific goal or cause. These types of registries are very popular among couples who are already stocked up on housewares and want to give guests a unique option for gifts. So what type of alternative registry best fits you and your bride-to-be? Consider the following options.

Honeymoon Registry

Are you worried about coming up with the cash to book your ultimate honeymoon? A honeymoon registry gives your guests the opportunity to contribute money directly into a post-wedding vacation travel fund. Typically, you're given a custom website to tell your friends and family about your travel plans and approximate budget. From there, they can use a credit or debit card to give their gift from the comfort of their own home. Either before or after the wedding, you can simply request a check from the company holding the funds. While these registries are usually online, I've come across more and more travel agents who are starting to offer similar services through their businesses.

Charity

Instead of asking for fine china or crystal you'll only use once a year (if that), why not consider using your wedding gift registry as a call-to-action for people to get involved with your favorite charity? Charity registries involve accepting cash donations toward a cause in lieu of physical gifts. It's a great way to use such a happy moment in your life to bring a little happiness to someone else in the world who really needs it. Besides, there isn't a pair of newlyweds in the world who couldn't use a little good karma.

Once you've decided on the charity you'd like to use, contact them and ask about their preferred method for setting up a registry. They'll most likely already have a system in place through their website. But they may ask you to collect the money yourself and make one large donation after the wedding. If that's the case, you'll need to let guests know that in lieu of gifts, you'll be accepting donations. The best way to do this is through your wedding website or the website of your charity. If you're comfortable sharing, it's always a nice gesture to explain why the specific charity you've chosen means so much to you. If you have a personal story or experience to share, your guests will appreciate hearing about it. Plus, it'll give them a better idea of how their money will help the cause.

Create-a-Gift

If you're saving money for a big purchase, such as a new car or a home, registries that can help you raise money are also available. A create-a-gift registry can be set up through your bank or credit card issuer. Similar to the honeymoon registry, it enables your guests to make contributions toward a large-scale item. There's power in numbers, and with your guests' generosity, you'll be able to afford these purchases much sooner than if you had saved on your own. Just be sure to remember your thank-you notes.

Bride's Gift and Wedding Bands

Congrats! Flipping to this chapter means you probably already have some of your major wedding planning details nailed down (if not, see Chapter 3 to start hashing out your wedding planning game plan). Now, it's time to start thinking about selecting two very important items: your wedding bands and the perfect gift for your lovely bride-to-be.

Whatever you do, don't wait until the last minute to start shopping for these essential items on your wedding checklist. Although it may seem like you're finally nearing the home stretch, you can't slack off now. But don't sweat it—once you knock these things off your list, you'll be one step closer to living out your boyhood dream of that magical wedding day.

One for My Baby: The Bride's Gift

By now, you're probably feeling like you've already dropped some serious coin on gifts for your wedding party and parents, not to mention most likely on the wedding itself. So I know what you're thinking: I have to give my fiancée a wedding gift, too?

I'll give it to you straight: the answer is yes. And make sure to take your time selecting this gift. It's an important one—especially to her, which, as you've no doubt learned by now, means it should be important to you as well (at least it's not floral arrangements this time, right?).

Failing to remember your bride's gift can result in taking the express route to the doghouse—and who wants that at the beginning of a marriage? (Trust me—there'll be plenty of time to land yourself in the doghouse later on.) But if you get this right and really impress her, you might just succeed in scoring some get-out-of-jail-free points with your bride for the first few months of marriage—and that's a gift you can both appreciate.

MAN DOWN
Don't take the easy way out and make the mistake of relying on a salesperson to help you come up with the "perfect" wedding gift for your bride. A stranger's tastes will likely be totally different than your fiancée's, resulting in an impersonal gift. Really think about what's meaningful to your bride or what her favorite things are and go from there. If all else fails, be sly about asking her what her dream gifts might be (say, when you're registering for wedding gifts).

Although it may seem a bit gratuitous (to you), giving your bride-to-be a wedding gift is not only an age-old tradition but also a meaningful gesture that she'll remember for years to come. The first step is to put a little thought into it. Whether your gift is traditional, sentimental, functional, or fun, it pays to take some time to think about what type of gift she'd truly enjoy or that would be meaningful to her. You've already hit a home run with an amazing marriage proposal, so now's the time to seal the deal with a kick-ass gift that will show her the romance is far from over as well as reinforce the fact that she's marrying the perfect guy.

Of course, by now you probably feel like you truly know your fiancée. You may even complete each other's sentences. But figuring out what kind of wedding gift she'd really love isn't always so easy.

Don't make the same mistake as the groom in the movie *Father of the Bride* by presenting your blushing bride with a blender. That little mistake resulted in her temporarily calling off the wedding. Remember, cooking-oriented or otherwise stereotypical "housewife" gifts almost always result in disappointed and angry brides (unless your fiancée considers herself to be the next Julia Child, in which case a culinary gadget may be a perfectly acceptable gift).

If you're not quite sure which kind of wedding gift would best suit your beautiful bride, here are a few excellent options to consider:

- **Traditional:** a piece of jewelry. Whether it's a pair of diamond earrings, a necklace, or a bracelet to complement her wedding rings, jewelry makes a perfect bride's gift. If she's not a diamond girl or finances are (understandably) tight so close to the wedding, consider other stones, such as pearls, or go with plain but elegant gold jewelry instead. Still out of your price range? Sterling silver is another great option.

- **Fun:** something for the honeymoon. While the honeymoon itself can be a wonderful gift to the bride, a gift that can be used on the honeymoon is another excellent choice. Ideas include getting her a new digital camera or camcorder to capture honeymoon memories or surprising her with an incredible honeymoon extra or excursion, such as a private dinner on the beach, a romantic couples massage, or a scenic waterfall tour by helicopter.

- **Sentimental:** write your own wedding vows. Channel your inner scribe and really show her how you feel about her by writing your own personal wedding vows for the big day. And if this is the kind of surprise you think she'd prefer to be in on beforehand (which is highly likely), let her know about it and she can write her own vows as well.

- **Functional:** a house down payment. While this may not be the sexiest gift, there's no doubt that this is a grand gesture that says you're truly in it for the long haul. Aside from your marriage proposal, nothing will show her you're ready to take this next important step in your lives like making a down payment on your first home together.

- **Sentimental:** a custom framed photo. Is her family, pet, or maybe even a childhood home really special to her? Have a photographer take a photo of them and have it professionally framed. Top it off by adding an engraved plaque with sentimental wording at the bottom. Another option: pay for the engagement photo session and have her favorite shot enlarged and framed for hanging in your home.

- **Fun:** a spa day. By now, her nerves are completely fried from all the wedding plans she's been working so hard on for the last few months. Let her relax and unwind for a day (maybe even during your honeymoon) by treating her to her favorite pampering spa treatments, such as a facial, massage, manicure/pedicure, or haircut.

- **Functional:** something related to her career or favorite hobby. For example, has she always wanted to go back to school and get her MBA? Pay for her first semester of tuition. Does she absolutely love cooking? Treat her to some cooking lessons with a famous chef or at a local culinary academy. Has she been thinking about scrapbooking your wedding memories? Offer to cover the cost of materials and scrapbooking classes to get her started.

- **Sentimental:** a bottle of wine to be opened on your fifth (or tenth, fifteenth, and so on) wedding anniversary. Show her you're in it for good by surprising her with a special bottle of wine to uncork in celebration of a future anniversary or another special occasion, such as the birth of your first child. Another idea: consider presenting her with a time capsule (in a small box or chest) containing keepsakes from your wedding (such as the invitation, monogrammed items, wedding favors, photos, and so on). She'll be amazed at your thoughtful gesture.

- **Functional and sentimental:** money to put toward a fifth or tenth anniversary trip. Or, consider setting up a special vacation fund that you can contribute to on a monthly basis. This is another gift that lets her know you're serious about spending the rest of your life with her and plan on celebrating your marriage's major milestones in style.

Although it may sound cheesy, in this case the thought really does count in the eyes of your fiancée. Whatever type of gift you decide on, your bride will love the fact that you made the effort to present her with a meaningful wedding gift.

CHA-CHING

If you want to give your bride a wedding gift but the steam's still coming off your wallet from all those extra wedding expenses, try going the sentimental route. For example, pour your heart out in an emotional letter for her to open on the wedding day or even on your first anniversary. Romantic gestures don't have to cost money, and she'll love the fact that you took the time to declare your true feelings on paper. Consider coupling it with a bouquet of her favorite flowers or chocolate.

If your gift ends up totally bombing, don't stress; there are always anniversaries and birthdays. Dust yourself off, and try your best to nail it next time.

Selecting Wedding Bands

That's right, guys: it's time to head back to the jeweler once again. But this time, you'll likely be picking out the last pieces of jewelry for a little while: your wedding bands. And just like purchasing the engagement ring, you should know that this is a very important decision. You'll both be wearing these bands for years to come, so you'll want to make sure you're happy with them. So naturally, as in many other areas of your wedding, it pays to shop around and see what options exist before committing.

If you're starting to freak out about your budget, relax. You most likely won't be expected to pick up the cost of both rings. According to etiquette, the groom traditionally pays for the bride's engagement and wedding rings, while the bride covers the cost of the groom's wedding band. But when it comes to budgeting, you can expect to spend anywhere from a few hundred to a few thousand, depending on the styles, metals, and jewels you choose.

Do I Have to Wear a Wedding Band?

Think you can manage to get away without having to wear a wedding band, big guy? Think again. Once you're committed, you have to go all in. No matter how progressive your fiancée may be, it's highly unlikely that she'll let something this important slide.

Although the idea of having to wear jewelry for the rest of your life is enough to make some guys' skin crawl, this is one piece of jewelry even the most macho men should sport with pride. Wearing your wedding band shows your commitment to one another, makes the wedding official (according to some religious denominations), and sends a signal to single ladies that you're officially off the market (sorry, but it's time to accept that fact).

To novice ring-wearers, at first it will feel strange—and you'll constantly fight the urge to twirl it around your finger or take it off and spin it like a top. But after you wear it for a few weeks, you'll get used to it and will forget you're even wearing it. Remember, your fiancée has already been wearing her engagement ring for months. Once the wedding day arrives, it's your turn to man up and follow suit.

When to Shop

So when should you start looking for wedding bands? The majority of jewelers typically recommend purchasing your bands at least two to four months prior to the wedding. You'll need to allow for some time to have your ring sized and adjusted after you purchase it, so it's important not to wait until the last minute to start shopping.

If you plan to have custom rings designed, you should start working with a jeweler as soon as possible—or at least six months before the wedding. Like a custom car, this type of ring will take a little extra time to create, so make sure to plan accordingly.

Shopping Tips

If you already purchased your fiancée's engagement ring as a set with her wedding band or she plans to wear an engagement ring alone, you can breathe easy and focus on finding your band. But if not, you'll need to dedicate time to shopping for both bands. Either way, you should plan to shop with your fiancée so you both can select bands that nicely complement each other.

As your bride-to-be will likely tell you, you shouldn't get a yellow-gold band if hers is made of white gold. While the bands don't have to match exactly (no guy wants a girly-looking ring), they should at least look like they belong to the same family—and, at a minimum, be made from the same color metal.

Initially, it may help to do some Internet research to see what types of wedding bands both you and your fiancée prefer before stepping into the jewelry store. Believe it or not, there are many different types of rings available (for both men and women), and determining which one works best for you may seem a bit overwhelming at first. Once you've had a chance to narrow down your preferences, you can better articulate your requirements to your jeweler, who can show you several options that meet your needs.

Metal Types and Colors

You have several metal options to consider when shopping for wedding bands, and the right ring will ultimately come down to your personal style and budget. Your jeweler will be able to best explain the differences between the available options, but here's a quick overview of some of today's most common metal choices.

Gold. This perennially popular option doesn't tarnish or rust and polishes to a brilliant shine. Too soft for everyday wear, pure gold is typically alloyed with other metals to increase its strength and durability. Gold has a natural yellow color but is alloyed with silver, nickel, or palladium to create white gold. Because the resulting metal has a yellow tint, white gold is often plated with rhodium to enhance its white color. This plating can wear off over time, requiring re-plating to restore its white tint. While gold is less durable than industrial metals, it can be easily engraved.

MAN UP
Want to impress your fiancée? Know your gold terminology, such as "karat." Karat refers to the purity of the gold. For example, 24k gold is 100 percent gold, and 18k gold is an alloy of 18 parts gold and 6 parts other metal.

Platinum. Another popular choice, platinum is a very durable metal, and its natural white tint doesn't tarnish. Platinum is rarer than gold, which means it's also more expensive. For those who have sensitive skin, it's hypoallergenic because it isn't alloyed with other metals. However, this metal is more easily scratched and weighs more than gold, making it feel heavier on the finger.

Palladium. Like platinum, palladium is a naturally white metal. It's also hypoallergenic and typically costs less than platinum and white gold. Palladium is quite a bit lighter than platinum as well as harder, which increases its durability.

Titanium. This very durable and lightweight industrial metal has a medium-gray color. Titanium doesn't tarnish and is hypoallergenic. It doesn't shine as much as gold, however.

Tungsten. Another hypoallergenic metal, tungsten is an industrial metal that sports a dark-gray color. Tungsten resists tarnish and scratches but is heavier than titanium.

Recycled metals. If you're looking for an eco-friendly option, check out recycled metals as well as conflict-free gemstones or diamonds.

Style and Finish

Your fiancée likely already has some ideas about what type of band she'd like to wear with her engagement ring. But if not, it may be helpful to have a conversation with your jeweler to see what types of bands might best complement her ring and to try on a few different options. It's typically best to choose the same metal and a style that's in keeping with that of the engagement ring. Her band may also include diamonds or other stones, depending on her tastes.

When it comes to your ring, the decision may not be as easy if you don't typically wear jewelry. A little advice: the style of your wedding band should reflect your personal taste and lifestyle. If you're a no-frills kind of guy, you'd sooner walk across a pit of steaming coals than wear a giant gleaming band encrusted with diamonds. Likewise, if you constantly dress to impress and like a bit of flash and glitz on a daily basis, a simple gold band just won't do it for you.

Your line of work may also be a factor in selecting your ring. If you work outside or with your hands the majority of the time, you'll probably want a simpler yet durable ring that isn't as prone to scratches and dings. If you work an office job, you won't have to worry about a larger, diamond-studded band getting in the way or taking a beating on a regular basis.

The good news is that whatever your taste and style may be, there's likely a perfect band out there for you if you take the time to look around. You'd be surprised at the vast range of options available when it comes to men's wedding bands. If you aren't able to find a few options that interest you by looks alone online or in a magazine, visit a jeweler, where you can actually try on some rings to see which types best suit you.

Popular men's ring finishes include: shiny/polished (brilliant and reflective), matte (the opposite of shiny; less reflective), satin (reflectivity between polished and matte), brushed (textured with visible brush strokes), and hammered (textured with small, pitted hammering marks). To add interest to a simpler ring, some men may prefer a milgrained look, which features a classic miniature beaded-edge design, or a two-toned look, which combines two different types or colors of metals.

Still looking for something a little different? Many, many other unique ring designs are available, such as those with an angular look, a woven pattern, or a Celtic design. Rings can also be engraved on the inside (with a sentiment that you and your wife share, for example) or outside for a completely different look. Shop around to find the one that best fits your own personal sense of style.

Add Some Bling

If you want to add some bling to your ring, you'll find many men's wedding band options that incorporate diamonds or other gemstones. Some rings have just a few diamonds or stones (solitaire, two stones, or three stones) on the front of the band, while others (multi-stone) sport diamonds or stones that encircle the entire ring.

Not into white diamonds? Bands can include many other jewels, such as black diamonds, sapphires, garnets, emeralds, or birthstones to add some glitz without sacrificing masculinity.

Size and Fit

When it comes to the size and fit of your wedding band, comfort is tantamount. It's important to try on the ring of your choice before committing to buying it. A ring may look great online or in the jeweler's case, but it may look too wide or narrow or drive you absolutely nuts once you slip it on your finger.

Fit is a very important consideration when buying your band. Fits range from classic to what's called a "comfort fit," which features rounded edges rather than straight-cut ones. This particular type of fit is worth a look because it won't dig into your skin and may feel a bit more comfortable for guys who aren't used to wearing rings.

The width of a wedding band is measured in millimeters, and men's bands are usually available in widths between 3mm and 8mm. You should try on a couple different widths to see which ones you prefer aesthetically or that feel the least constricting on your finger. The wider the band, the more you'll feel it.

Also, make sure that the bands you select are resizable. Several factors, including changes in the seasons and weight fluctuation, can cause your wedding band to become too tight or loose over time. Ask your jeweler whether the ring size can be adjusted accordingly, if necessary.

Ring Insurance

Once you've pulled the trigger and purchased a killer set of wedding bands, don't forget about insurance. You'd be surprised by how many men (and women) manage to lose their bands as early as during the honeymoon (while swimming, for example), so make sure your rings are covered as soon as you buy them.

MAN DOWN

When purchasing insurance for your wedding bands, keep in mind that normal wear and tear, scratches, and re-plating most likely won't be covered by insurance. Do your best to treat your rings with care, and realize that you may need to spend some extra money down the road to restore them to their original beauty.

You'll find plenty of insurance options for your bands, depending on your specific needs and situation. For example, you can add a jewelry clause to your existing homeowner's or renter's insurance policy. Alternatively, many insurance companies specialize in covering jewelry— or your jeweler may even offer in-house insurance coverage you can purchase until you're ready to make a long-term decision.

Before you choose a policy, make sure to ask exactly what's covered (theft/loss, stones falling out, and so on) and at what amount. Don't just settle for the cheapest policy without analyzing the benefits involved. Remember, you've put a lot of time and money into these rings, so don't overlook this last step of the process. Make sure you have a good insurance policy, so if the worst happens and you need to replace them, you'll be covered.

7

Style and Attire

I'd like to make an addendum to the old saying, "You are what you eat." In many cases, you're also what you wear. This statement couldn't be more appropriate for your wedding day. Your choice of attire, along with your overall look, feel, and style, will be the lasting impression your wedding photos will capture. Whether you're more of a Don Draper or a Zach Galifianakis, planning your wedding attire and style choices to match who you are personalizes your wedding while creating lifelong memories.

By looking and feeling your best on your wedding day, you're also ensuring greater confidence. As the groom, you'll be standing in front of your friends and family as (one of the two) centers of attention. If you have experience with public speaking, you know that you can't be successful without confidence. Being confident is also key to being *the man*. And by taking the time to get your wedding style right, you'll not only be doing yourself a favor but also giving your bride the real-life fairytale wedding she has always dreamed about. So make sure to do it right, fellas.

Attire

As with all major wedding decisions, attire choices should be a team effort. Starting around six months before the wedding date, or as soon as your bride has chosen her gown and bridesmaid dresses, you should begin coordinating with her on the attire choices for the groom's side. By this point, the wedding colors will have been selected and you can start looking at shirt, vest, and tie options that match those colors. It's important to relinquish some control to your fiancée here, even in terms of what you'll be wearing. Don't fool yourself into thinking that the tux colors will drive the entire color scheme for the wedding. That's far from true.

Tux Versus Suit

The first major attire-related decision that you and your fiancée will make is whether the groom and groomsmen will be wearing tuxedos or suits on the wedding day. Taste definitely comes into play here; however, this decision will primarily hinge on how formal your wedding will be. A formal church wedding almost always calls for the groom's side of the wedding party to wear tuxedos. However, for a semiformal wedding, a dark suit with an off-white shirt is a popular choice.

 CHA-CHING
If you opt to buy a tuxedo, get yourself a quality one. While you'll probably spend close to $1,000, it will pay for itself in multiple uses. With a cheaper option, you'll run the risk of having to buy a replacement when it doesn't hold up after multiple wears and cleanings.

Renting Versus Owning

When you're deciding whether to rent or buy your tux or suit, estimate the number of future events where you could potentially wear the attire again to help justify the heftier purchase. Does your line of work require you to attend a lot of black-tie events, for example?

If you don't expect to wear it again within the next couple years, you'll save money by renting rather than purchasing. Of course, if you opt to purchase your tux or suit, there's no doubt that you'll feel great in your attire—and that will show in your posture. My only advice: if you're planning to buy, make sure to purchase something that's more classic and traditional instead of loud and trendy so it will stay in style for years to come.

Remember that if you rent, you'll most likely only spend about a third of the cost of buying a new suit or tux. And you won't feel obligated to wear a tux or suit that you purchased just because you spent all that money on it.

Non-Formal Options

Having a less-formal event or a destination wedding? This allows you some extra freedom with your attire choices. We've all seen photos from beach weddings where everyone is in white dress shirts, khakis, and flip-flops. There's a reason why this scenario is so common: it's a great look. The "beach" look can actually work well for any outdoor wedding, no matter how close the nearest body of water is.

You can also have some non-traditional fun with your shoes. If you're getting married in her parents' church, it's probably not a good idea to break out the Chuck Taylor All-Stars. However, if your wedding is in a less-formal setting, have at it. You can also get creative with your ties and color of suits (baby blue, anyone?).

Accessories

Wedding-day attire comes with its fair share of accessories. In fact, it's a lot to keep track of. If you're a formal-wear novice, the concepts of cummerbunds, ascots, and cuff links will leave your head spinning. The main thing to know is that accessories add personality and flash to you and your groomsmen's attire.

Here's a cheat sheet on the most common pieces:

- Your tie selection is dictated by your choice of tuxedo or suit. Tuxes usually are worn with a standard bowtie that matches the jacket color. For less-formal weddings, neckties are fair game as long as they go with your shirt and wedding colors.

- Although small, cuff links play a big part in any formal look. However, they're a pain in the ass to put on, so don't be afraid to recruit your father or best man to help. If you're still in the market for groomsmen gifts, consider buying yourself and your groomsmen matching sets to wear on the big day.

- The popularity of *Mad Men* has brought pocket squares back into the limelight. They can inject a little pop of color into your look, which is rarely a bad thing. If using one, match it to your tie or shirt color.

- Yeah, yeah, yeah, I know you're not big on flowers. However, the boutonnière is a staple look for the groom. Select one that matches your bride's bouquet and is different from the ones being worn by your groomsmen so you'll stand out a bit.

- The first question guys have about cummerbunds is, "What the heck are they?" A cummerbund is a pleated waist sash that's often worn with tuxedos. If your wedding is formal, you might want to consider this accessory because it provides a touch of class to the look.

- If you're renting attire, your rental shop will also offer matching shoes. However, you're not tied to their choice. Some grooms will buy themselves new shoes for the wedding day. For formal weddings, black leather shoes work best. However, if your wedding is a little more casual, there's nothing wrong with brown, white, or any other color that matches your attire. Just remember to also coordinate the color of your socks. You don't want everyone pointing out that you can't wear brown socks with black shoes.

The Fitting Process

For tuxedo rentals, it's extremely important to be organized not only with your measurement process but also with your groomsmen's. After you decide what you'll be wearing and where you'll be renting from, you should schedule a group fitting for you and the wedding party. This fitting should also include both your father and your future father-in-law.

No one likes walking into a tux shop to waste 30 minutes, but this can actually be a fun experience. A group fitting allows all the guys to get together. You might even make a day of it and hit the golf course afterward. You can schedule a second fitting if necessary, but usually those who can't make the first fitting can stop in on their own time. For friends in other cities, let them know that they can get measured locally and then call in their measurements to the store where you'll be renting.

Also, make sure to inform everyone about the cutoff date for turning in their measurements and deposits. In fact, you might even consider giving them a fake deadline that's a few days before the real deadline to help ensure that any habitually late people will still make the actual deadline. The shop's deadline will usually be two months before the scheduled pickup; otherwise, the shop can't guarantee that the tuxedos will be available and in stock on the wedding date. One month before the wedding, call the tux shop to verify the pickup date and time and to make sure they have everyone's deposits.

MAN UP
Depending on how many tuxes you'll be renting, you're likely to receive one or two free rentals as part of your package. While it would certainly be nice to use the freebie on yourself, consider gifting it to your dad or hers. It'll be a much-appreciated gesture and sign of respect.

A few days before the wedding, you and the other wedding party members will need to stop in to pick up your tuxes. It's very important for everyone to try theirs on at this time to see whether any last-minute alterations are necessary. Everyone should also double check that all the appropriate pieces and accessories are there. You don't want your best man to get stuck without shoes or cuff links, do you?

Standing Out

It's no secret that your bride is going to shine on the big day. How could she not? But have you given any thought to how you can make yourself stand out from the other members of the wedding party? It's easy for the groom and groomsmen to all look alike in their penguin suits. But because this is your wedding day, I urge you to strive beyond simply blending in. After deciding what your attire style is, start playing around with different options. The bride and her family will definitely have some input, but they'll be impressed that you're taking it upon yourself to get the initial research done.

If your wedding party is wearing tuxedos, for example, it's customary for the groom to wear a different vest color that designates him as the main man. Go with a completely different color instead of just changing the shade. For example, if the groomsmen are wearing black vests, go with white or ivory for yourself. The same goes for boutonnières. Consider going with a different size, color, and type of flower. If you really feel like standing out, more and more men are opting to go with a completely different suit or tux color than everyone else. This is a bold statement but one that can really distinguish you from the pack.

Cost-Saving Tips

Let's face it: cost is an overriding issue in every wedding. And in the case of groom and groomsmen attire, the bills can add up quickly. It can be stressful knowing that you and your wolf pack have to foot the bill for attire rental or purchase, especially if you're unsure of everyone's financial standing. The last thing you want is one of your groomsmen not being able to participate in the wedding because he can't afford the tux rental you've chosen.

To help keep as much money as possible in everyone's pockets, consider these ideas for keeping attire as affordable as possible:

- Wear your own suits instead of renting or buying them.
- Allow the groomsmen to have only matching ties or shirts.
- Browse the Internet for deals on formal wear.
- Shop around for stores that offer discounts on group rentals or purchases. In our Groupon-like times, there's buying power in numbers.

One Groom's Story:
Lawrence in Memphis

Planning a wedding from afar always presents challenges. While you can mitigate many of these issues with careful planning, unexpected problems can often arise at the last minute. This was the case with Lawrence from Memphis, Tennessee, who was planning to marry his bride three hours away in Nashville.

All five of Lawrence's groomsmen also lived in Memphis but planned to rent tuxedos from a shop in Nashville. Everyone had gone through the process of being fitted back home and faxing their measurements across the state to the tux shop. The plan was for everyone to arrive in Nashville on Friday morning to pick up their tuxes, which would leave ample time for any last-minute alterations before the Saturday wedding.

Unfortunately, as often happens, one of the groomsmen was running late. He had been caught up at work and then ran into a mega traffic jam on his way out of Memphis. He called ahead to let Lawrence know that someone would have to grab his tux for him as he would be pushing it to even make it to the rehearsal on time. With some trepidation, Lawrence grabbed the tux and prayed it would fit. But of course, it didn't. There was a discrepancy in the measurements, and the jacket was two sizes too small. To make matters worse, by the time the problem was discovered, the tux shop had already closed for the weekend. Luckily for Lawrence, one of the bridesmaids happened to know the owner of the tux shop and was able to get him to open the shop on Saturday morning to switch out the new jacket before the wedding.

This story represents an extremely close call that all grooms can learn from. If you're planning an out-of-town wedding, sit down and have a brainstorming session with your fiancée about anything and every-thing that could go wrong, especially in relation to attire. You can never be too prepared. In this scenario, the wedding party could have rented tuxes at home and taken them to Nashville. Or, the couple could have asked the wedding party to arrive on Thursday instead of Friday to avoid any last-minute issues. Lawrence came close to having a groomsman without a tux jacket on the wedding day. Don't let this happen to you or I promise you'll never hear the end of it.

Getting in Shape

On the wedding day, she'll be expecting you to be her knight in shining armor. But what if you currently look more like the court jester than Sir Lancelot? It's easy to put off starting a workout routine and getting yourself in shape. Gym memberships and personal trainers are expensive, and busy schedules don't often allow much extra time to take on a new activity (especially during the wedding-planning months). However, if you've always wanted to get into an exercise routine, your wedding day can serve as the perfect goal.

Unless you're a '90s-era Major League Baseball player, building muscle and trimming fat takes time. There really is no overnight path to success. The hardest part of the process is getting started and knowing what to do. I strongly recommend consulting with a doctor or trainer before starting any program, but here are a few basic guidelines to get you moving in the right direction:

- Start by figuring out where you currently stand. Do you need a complete overhaul, or are you only looking to add a few pounds of muscle? If you get winded walking up and down stairs, you may be looking at a more serious issue that you should discuss with a doctor.

- Design a program that's right for you. This can be as simple as running and weight training every other day or as complex as joining a boot-camp program that puts you through an NFL training camp–type workout every morning.

- If you're going to be working out at home, search the Internet for some equipment. Often, simple items such as weights, medicine balls, or even a jump rope might be all you need. However, if you're looking to get into complex equipment or machinery, make sure to do some research. Additionally, workout videos such as P90X are designed to be used in the comfort of your own living room and are worth considering.

- No pain, no gain. It's so important to follow through and be honest with yourself by sticking to your workout. There's really no point in starting a regular routine if you're not going to stick to it.

- Monitor your progress on a weekly basis. I recommend keeping a journal that details changes in weight, pulse, body mass index (BMI), and new achievements such as being able to run two miles without stopping.

If your bride-to-be is also planning on starting a pre-wedding workout routine or ramping up her existing workouts, why not consider joining forces and building muscle together? Working out can be a great couple's activity, not to mention help combat some of the wedding-planning stress you've both been facing. Whether it's joining a gym, regular jogging, or experimenting with some strenuous positions in the bedroom, burning fat feels better when you do it together.

Health and Skin Care

Getting yourself in shape isn't really worth it if you're not going to look after your overall health as well. In addition to working out, being mindful of your health should be part of your wedding preparations. This starts by maintaining a good diet (which should be part of your normal life anyway).

The most logical place to start is cutting fast-food from your diet. I understand how convenient the lure of the drive-thru is. And hey, the food is damn good, too. However, dangerous fat is lurking within every bite of a cheeseburger or French fry.

It's tough to change your eating habits overnight, so here are five tips for getting yourself started on healthier eating:

- As a substitute for greasy meats, eat more fish.
- Finish all your vegetables (and perhaps ask for seconds).

- Don't eat right before going to bed; it's unhealthy for your body to digest food as you snooze.

- Instead of eating due to stress, turn your frustration into positive energy by going for a walk or light jog.

- Cut your alcohol intake by limiting yourself to only a few drinks per week.

Your skin is another area that can use some extra attention before the wedding—especially if you struggle with acne and don't want any blemishes popping up in wedding photos. The easiest way to keep your skin clear is by getting into a habit of washing your face both in the morning and before you go to bed at night. There are plenty of over-the-counter treatments that you can use in conjunction with your regular bathing. You might even consider asking your fiancée if she uses any kind of moisturizer or face wash. If she does, try it out for a few weeks and see whether it provides results. For extreme cases, you might want to pay your dermatologist a visit a few months before the wedding to see whether he or she can prescribe a more powerful face wash. There's nothing to be ashamed of with acne. Most adults (myself included) struggle with this issue their entire lives.

Hair

Take a look at your parents' wedding album. Notice anything funny? I'm not talking about the vintage tuxes and bridesmaid dresses (which are indeed hilarious)—but rather the hairstyles and facial hair of the groom and male members of the wedding party. Are there any mullets or mutton-chop sideburns floating around? My guess is yes. Take a moment to laugh and poke a few jabs at your old man, and then stop to remind yourself that unless you make wise style choices, your kids might be doing the same to you in 20 years. You, and especially your bride, should want your wedding photos to be timeless and not date your wedding to a time period or style that later crashed and burned. Can you say faux hawk?

Of course, every guy has his own personal hair style. I'm certainly not asking you to buzz your hair off if shagginess has always been your thing. I'm also not saying that you need to go clean-shaven if you're a beard guy. However, when it comes to your hair on the wedding day, it's best to be a bit conservative. You can still be you, but just be a *cleaner* you. Schedule a haircut for two weeks before the wedding date. This will allow your locks time to grow into the style, because hair seldom looks exactly how you want it to immediately after being cut. A few days before the wedding, stop back in for a last-minute trim and shave. Hell, if your barber offers a straight-razor shave, treat yourself. This is something that every man should experience at some point in his life. Your wedding is the perfect excuse to try it.

MAN UP
Do some pre-wedding bonding with your boys at a grooming lounge or barber shop, where you can all get haircuts, shaves, massages, and even manicures—all accompanied with Scotch. This is a great way to kick off your bachelor party or wedding weekend. The outing could also serve as part of your thank-you gift to your groomsmen.

I also recommend encouraging your wedding party to give their stylists a visit as well or taking them all to a men's grooming lounge as a grooms-man gift or pre-wedding outing. Give them the same guidelines that you're giving yourself. While you can't force someone to clean up their style, you can tell them that their groomsman gift might be returned if they don't.

Wedding Planning Duties for Dudes

Although it may sound far-fetched, there are actually some things grooms can really get into during the wedding-planning process. While your fiancée may understandably take the reins on selecting wedding-related items such as the place settings, linens, and flowers (no arguments here, right?), there are many other areas where you can—and should—add your two cents, if not take the lead and tackle yourself.

Just a few of these man-friendly areas include the wedding entertainment (DJ, band, and so on), the groom's cake (yes, there's a cake just for you!), the wedding-day transportation (who doesn't love a sweet ride?), the wedding ceremony, and the reception.

What Grooms Need to Know

While grooms of past generations (such as your dad or grandfather, for example) may have traditionally sat back, put up their feet, and gladly let their brides-to-be handle 100 percent of the wedding-planning duties, today's grooms are different. No longer keen to simply show up per instructions on the wedding day, modern grooms want their voices to be heard as well. And why shouldn't they? Not only are they likely paying for at least some portion of the wedding festivities themselves, but they also want to be involved in the planning process and help put their own personal stamp on the event. After all, a wedding is the celebration of *two* people uniting as a couple, right?

TRADITION SAYS
According to tradition, the bride's family covered the cost of the wedding ceremony and reception, but of course that's not always the case now. Today, the couple's families may split some of the costs of these events, or the couple may jointly pay for the ceremony and reception on their own.

Guys, this is your chance to add your personal touch to one of the most important occasions in your life. Don't sit back and let it pass you by. Your wedding shouldn't be all about your bride; it should be about *both* of you.

Wedding Entertainment

What guy doesn't like to plan a killer party? This is your chance to get the party started just the way you like it by selecting the perfect entertainment for your wedding reception. Whether you prefer a DJ or a professional band, the decisions you make here will set the mood for the reception, get people dancing, and ensure that everyone has a great time celebrating your wedding.

While you and your bride will have an amazing time at your reception no matter what happens (it's your day, after all), it's important to remember that the music and dance floor atmosphere can easily make or break the reception. Don't disappoint them by letting the entertainment become an afterthought. Get involved early: plan to book reception entertainment six to nine months prior to your wedding date, and choose an entertainer who best suits the tastes of you and your guests.

DJ Versus Band

Ah, the age-old dilemma: Should we have a DJ or band at our wedding reception? Which one's best for you and your fiancée? It really depends on your personal preferences, tastes, and ultimately, your budget. While you and your bride-to-be may love bluegrass, for example, your guests may not be so easy to please. To keep your guests on the dance floor all night long, it pays to think about the advantages that both of these options can offer.

Not sure which type of entertainment is right for your reception? Here are some tips to help you decide:

Bands

What you'll love:

- Live music is tough to beat.

- If you love one particular genre or style of music, there's likely a band out there that specializes in it or that can cater to your needs. (Just make sure the music style appeals to a wide range of people so you don't end up alienating your guests.)

- Live performers can personalize songs according to their own musical abilities, revise or add new lyrics, or slow down your favorite up-tempo song and make it sound completely different.

- Bands can "read" the room and adjust the tempo accordingly or cater to certain themes you may want to incorporate.

- Some bands will learn a couple of new songs per your request (although possibly at an extra charge).

What to consider:

- A band's repertoire is typically limited, depending on their specialty and the instruments they incorporate.

- If you're set on using specific songs for your dances, such as your first dance or mother-son dance, and the band doesn't already know it or doesn't have time to learn it, you may have to select another song or play a CD of the song instead.

- When the band goes on break—typically every two hours or so— the mood can suffer. However, recorded music will likely be played in between.

- Bands are typically more expensive than DJs. You'll be paying for several musicians and their time, rather than one DJ. Also, keep in mind that all of the band members will need to be served dinner.

DJs

What you'll love:

- DJs typically play an incredibly wide range of music (from the '60s all the way to today's latest hits, for example) that can be tailored to your tastes.

- No breaks in the music. A DJ will continuously play tunes all night long to keep guests entertained throughout the entire reception.

- Requested songs are the real thing, rather than covered by imitators.

- A DJ who can strike a balance between being serious and humorous can be very entertaining. While the music's playing, he or she can work the room to get guests fired up and out on the dance floor.

- Like bands, DJs can read the room and adjust the tempo accordingly.

- DJs are typically less expensive than live bands.

What to consider:

- The risk of equipment failure is a possibility. Make sure the DJ you select has several backup procedures in place beforehand.

- A cheesy, extremely loud, or obnoxious DJ can be a real turn-off for many guests.

- Guests are more apt to ask a DJ to play songs you may not love or feel are appropriate for your wedding. Create a "no-play" list to ensure that inappropriate songs aren't played, no matter who requests them.

Choosing the Right Entertainer

Before hiring either a band or a DJ, take time to see them perform live if at all possible. That way, you'll see them in their element and will know exactly what to expect when they play at your reception. If that isn't feasible, request a sample CD or DVD so you can see how they performed at another event. At a minimum, ask your band or DJ for references. Chatting with other satisfied customers can give you peace of mind in the form of a first-hand account of how things went and whether there were any regrets.

Also, make sure to carefully review your entertainer's contract before signing it so you're aware of everything you're agreeing to and know what to expect. For example, will the entertainer be there for the entire reception or only between certain hours? What will he or she do in the event of an equipment failure, illness, or other emergency? Are there any extra charges you should be aware of? Can he or she be paid overtime if necessary? Is the entertainer insured in case any equipment is damaged or goes missing? The contract should answer all these questions.

$ CHA-CHING

No room left in the budget for wedding entertainment? Look no further than your iPod and a nice set of speakers. Stock your MP3 player with the perfect playlist of dance tunes ahead of time, and get the party started without breaking the bank. Word of advice: have a buddy man it during the reception so he can go from one playlist to the next, if necessary, or switch up music styles if people aren't feeling the current vibe. (See Appendix B for playlist suggestions.)

A band or DJ should also allow you to provide a playlist of songs you and your fiancée want to hear as well as a no-play list of songs you absolutely don't want to be played, regardless of whether guests request them. While "The Thong Song" may have been your best man's favorite jam in college, requesting it at your wedding could send your bride into a fury as well as appall your grandmother. The same goes for songs such as "The Chicken Dance." Most couples either love these or hate these. Make sure to put any no-no tunes on your no-play list to ensure that only the type of music you deem appropriate is played during the reception. In addition, if you want to include special dances (such as a dollar dance or wedding party dance) during your reception, clue in your entertainer ahead of time so he or she can plan accordingly.

Beyond playing music, your band or DJ will likely also serve as the emcee of your reception, keeping your timeline on track (such as announcing your arrival, when it's time for your first dance, or cake-cutting time) and moving things along when necessary. Discuss your preferred timeline with your entertainer in advance to make sure everyone's on the same page to keep things running smoothly.

Cost and Gratuity

Like other areas of your wedding, the cost of your reception entertainment can range from hundreds to thousands, depending on the type of entertainment you select, what you expect of them, and any special extras you want to include. And while hiring a live band typically costs more than a DJ, this may not always be the case—so make sure to check around.

What about tipping? While it's optional, your entertainer will expect it, especially if you're happy with your entertainment's services or felt he or she exceeded your expectations. Although it's unlikely in this case, first check your contract to see whether gratuity is included. If not, plan to have your best man or other designated person deliver the gratuity at the end of the reception. Expect to tip musicians $20 to $25 each and tip DJs $50 to $100 (or 15 to 20 percent of their fee). Just keep in mind that tipping isn't required, especially if you're not happy with the services provided.

The Groom's Cake

That's right, guys—there's a special cake that's created just for you on your wedding day, known as the groom's cake. Usually provided by the groom and his family, this smaller (typically one-tier) cake can complement the larger, main wedding cake during the wedding reception or even be served as a special rehearsal dinner dessert. You should plan to order this cake at the same time as the main wedding cake (six to nine months prior to the wedding) or shortly thereafter.

Choosing a Cake to Suit Your Style

While the traditional wedding cake may incorporate colors from your wedding, flowers, pearls, or even resemble your bride's wedding dress, the groom's cake is a lot less fussy and much more macho. This cake focuses specifically on the groom, highlighting personal interests such as a favorite hobby, sports team, alma mater, much-loved pet, hometown, or career.

For example, if you're a die-hard pro or college football fan, your groom's cake could display your favorite team's logo, team colors, or mascot. Do you love to golf? Your cake could display your favorite course or resemble a golf club, or even depict the perfect hole-in-one. Love to fish on the weekends? Your cake could look like a beautiful big-mouthed bass. Is music your life? Have a cake designed to resemble your favorite instrument.

MAN UP
No room for a groom's cake on the table at the wedding reception? Consider serving it at the rehearsal dinner instead. The groom's family is likely already paying for this event, so it makes sense to serve it as a dessert here. It may even turn out to be less expensive than your caterer's dessert options.

The groom's cake can also be a bit more bold or creative when it comes to flavors, fillings, and icing. While the main wedding cake may offer more traditional flavors and fillings that the majority of your guests would enjoy, the groom's cake can feature less-expected flavors, such as peanut butter, pineapple, coconut cream, or rhubarb. Whatever you decide, consider using a flavor that's different than one used in the main wedding cake to give guests another option to enjoy.

The base of the groom's cake can also serve as a perfect spot to include any extras you'd like to include, such as chocolate-covered strawberries, your favorite kind of candy, or a special hometown treat. Guys, this is your chance to go nuts and personalize your cake as you see fit!

Cost

The cost of your groom's cake will likely depend on its size, complexity, and any extras you choose to throw in. While some bakeries charge a flat rate, others charge by the slice. Your bakery (or your reception venue or caterer) may also offer to slice and serve your cake for an extra fee. Make sure that delivery is included in your contract unless you plan to have someone pick up and deliver the cake for you.

Wedding-Day Transportation

Wedding-day transportation is another topic that most grooms can get excited about. The groom is traditionally financially responsible for arranging transportation for the newly married couple from the wedding reception to the hotel, airport, or other destination after the celebration has ended.

Whether you live for a certain type of car or simply want to leave your wedding reception in style, the transportation you select is an important decision—one you can have a blast arranging. You'll likely find many transportation options available, depending on your wedding location.

Popular Transportation Choices

Here's a quick overview of some of the most popular choices:

- **Traditional limousine.** This traditional yet classy option is a perennial favorite. Some limos come with tricked-out interiors as well, if that's how you like to roll.

- **Classic car.** Another classy choice, these cars can include a classic Rolls-Royce, Bentley, or Packard.

- **Stretch SUV.** Popular choices include stretch Hummers, Cadillac Escalades, and Ford Excursions.

- **Sports car.** Many transportation providers offer high-end sports cars, such as Ferraris, Lamborghinis, Maseratis, or Aston Martins. Know someone who collects cars? Ask whether you can borrow it for the occasion, possibly in lieu of a wedding gift.

- **Horse-drawn carriage.** This is a perfect option for the bride who has been dreaming of a fairy-tale wedding. Give her the royal treatment with this classy option.

- **Helicopter or boat.** Depending on your reception location, you could even leave your reception in a helicopter or boat to really blow your guests away and solidify your baller status.

Remember, you'll likely only be limited by your imagination and availability here, so do some research to make your ideal choice happen.

Cost and Gratuity

The cost of wedding transportation will depend on the type of vehicle you select, the hours you plan to have it reserved, and any extras you want to add, such as champagne, strawberries, flowers, or a red carpet leading to it. While most providers will include a "Just Married" sign posted in the back window (or wherever appropriate) in the cost, make sure to ask about it if you want it—or ask whether you can provide one if they don't offer it.

With transportation, an hourly rate, fuel, and gratuity (typically about 15 to 20 percent of the bill) will most likely be included in your contract. However, if you feel your provider went above and beyond, feel free to offer an additional tip. Also, expect to put down a deposit to reserve your selected vehicle in advance, with the remainder of the bill to be paid just prior to the wedding.

CHA-CHING
Want to have some extras, such as champagne, strawberries, or flowers, waiting for your bride in the chariot after the reception? These items can often be costly if purchased through your transportation provider; instead, ask whether you can buy them yourself and drop them off ahead of time to save some money.

When should you book? Plan to reserve your transportation at least four to six months prior to your wedding. Also, keep in mind that the most popular cars will be in high demand, especially during the busier spring and summer wedding months, so make sure to book your selection as early as possible. Also, plan to reserve rare or obscure cars as soon as possible, because fewer providers in your area may offer them.

The Wedding Ceremony

Naturally, you should expect to jointly plan the wedding ceremony with your fiancée. The type of ceremony and setting you choose will most likely depend on both of your religious beliefs, family expectations, or individual personalities.

This is one of the first items you'll need to book for your wedding and will most likely also determine your wedding date. Make sure to reserve your ceremony location as soon as possible (10 to 12 months prior to your wedding) to ensure availability.

Religious Ceremonies

If you both were brought up in religious homes (practicing or non-practicing), attend religious services on a regular basis, or feel that religion should be an integral part of your wedding, holding your ceremony in a place of worship is a natural choice. You might choose to have your wedding in the church, synagogue, or mosque you were raised in or in another place of worship that you currently attend; either way, incorporating religion in your ceremony can be very meaningful to you as a couple as well as to your family members.

What about interfaith marriages? According to tradition, couples are typically married in the bride's faith, but that decision is yours to make together. Many interfaith couples find a way to combine religious rituals in their ceremony. If you're Christian and your fiancée is Jewish, for example, consider combining elements of both religions in your ceremony. Or, if you're Catholic and your fiancée is Methodist, consider holding the ceremony in your fiancée's church but having your priest present to handle a portion of the ceremony, such as the exchange of rings. This is a great example of one of the many compromises you'll have to make together as you become a married couple.

Civil Ceremonies

Of course, if you and your fiancée can't agree on an appropriate interfaith arrangement, don't have a religious affiliation, or prefer to have a non-religious event, you can have a civil ceremony. In this type of ceremony, you can be married by a justice of the peace, mayor, judge, county clerk, notary public, or even a family member or close friend. Just make sure that the officiant can legally perform your ceremony if you want it to be recognized as a legal union.

This type of event also offers more freedom in terms of using non-traditional readings, music, and other ceremony elements than some religious denominations would allow in a traditional ceremony. Civil ceremonies can be held in an indoor venue such as city hall, a restaurant, an historical site, or in an outdoor location such as a beach, botanical garden, or mountain top.

Indoors Versus Outdoors

Deciding to hold your wedding ceremony indoors or outdoors likely depends on your personal preference, the location of your wedding, and the time of year you plan to have it. Of course, if you choose to have a religious wedding ceremony, you might not have the option of being married outside because some denominations require that you marry inside the place of worship. However, if you're able to choose either an indoor or outdoor location, make sure to compare the advantages and disadvantages to see which option makes the most sense for your wedding.

MAN DOWN
Even if you both agree about the type of wedding ceremony you'd like to have, don't just assume that you're both on the same page with all the details. Discuss your views on the ceremony with your fiancée ahead of time. There may be traditions you're unfamiliar with and would prefer not to include in your ceremony (such as including wording like "obey" or "'til death do us part" in your vows), or she may be planning to skip something you feel is essential. Talk it over beforehand to make sure you both agree on a game plan.

Holding your ceremony indoors or outdoors can be equally beautiful and memorable depending on the setting. While some couples don't mind planning an outdoor wedding at the risk of having to move everything indoors or under a tent if weather becomes an issue, others may not feel comfortable leaving their plans up to chance.

If you're set on a particular outdoor location, make sure to have a backup option in place in case it happens to rain, snow, or becomes dangerously windy during your ceremony. While a little adventure might not bother you and your fiancée, you should consider the safety of your guests. You don't want your 80-year-old grandmother to be stuck in the middle of an open field during a thunderstorm.

Cost and Gratuity

If you're planning to hold your wedding ceremony in a house of worship, you'll most likely be charged a fee to cover the service and the clergy's time. Expect to put down a deposit to reserve the date and pay the remainder just prior to the wedding day.

In some cases, if you already regularly donate money to the house of worship, your ceremony fee may be waived or discounted. However, if no fee is charged, a donation (typically a minimum of $100 up to $500 or more) is typically expected or requested. Most likely, the donation amount will be listed in your contract—but if not, ask what amount is appropriate. Although tipping the clergy is optional, a tip of $50 to $100 is a nice gesture (to be delivered by your best man on the day of the wedding). If travel is required, also expect to cover these costs for your officiant.

For civil ceremonies, tipping isn't necessary because these officials are typically paid a flat rate. While some civil officiants may appreciate donations, others may not legally be able to accept tips or donations. Discuss the appropriate protocol with them beforehand.

Ceremony Music

Most couples like to incorporate some type of music in the wedding ceremony. This is a great way to include songs that are meaningful to you and your fiancée, whether they're hymns or other sentimental songs. Just make sure to check with your officiant ahead of time to see whether the songs you'd like to include are allowed or appropriate. Ceremony entertainment can include organists, vocalists, string quartets, guitarists, pianists, or other musicians.

Most ceremony musicians or vocalists charge a flat fee for their services. If you're using an organist from your house of worship, check your ceremony contract to see whether his or her fee is already included. If not, expect to tip your organist $25 to $50 for his or her services. Also, expect to tip each musician or vocalist $25 to $50. Your best man should handle delivering these gratuities just after the ceremony.

Tastefully Including Pets

Want to include Fido in your wedding, but you or your fiancée are afraid it will appear tacky? Don't worry; there are plenty of tasteful ways to incorporate pets in your wedding ceremony. Just make sure to have someone on hand who can deliver the animal back home or to a neighbor's house once his or her role in the ceremony is over.

Here are a few pet-friendly wedding options to consider:

- **Man's best friend as ring bearer.** If you have a very well-trained dog (or other animal), he or she might be able to walk down the aisle with a ring pillow strapped to his or her back (and the rings attached with safety pins) or with the rings safely hung from a small bag or box attached to the collar. (Just make sure they're very securely attached to the animal just before the strut down the aisle to prevent any mishaps.)

- **Pet as accessory to human ring bearer or flower girl.** If your pet is super friendly, calm, and loves kids, consider having your ring bearer or flower girl walk your pet down the aisle to deliver your rings.

- **Pet as accessory to human groomsman or bridesmaid.** If you have a larger or less-mature pet, have an older wedding party member (such as a groomsman or bridesmaid) walk your pet down the aisle to keep him or her in check.

MAN UP

Has your fiancée put the kibosh on having a pet participate in your ceremony? Have a photo taken of the two of you together with your pet during your engagement photo session and display it in an appropriate place during the reception. Your pet may not be able to attend your wedding in person, but this tribute to him or her will let your guests know that your pet is an important family member who's there in spirit.

The Wedding Reception

The wedding reception venue is another major decision you and your fiancée will make while planning your big day. Along with your ceremony location, the reception venue is one of the first wedding details you'll need to book (typically 10 to 12 months before your wedding), which will likely also determine your wedding date.

Choosing a Venue and Caterer

The reception venue you select will depend on your personal tastes as well as its capability to accommodate your guests and needs. Some factors that will likely influence your decision are as follows:

- **Size/capacity.** Your venue must be large enough to comfortably accommodate all of your guests but not so large that it makes your wedding seem small.

- **Catering or food and beverage options.** You should love the venue's food and beverage offerings or be able to bring in a trusted caterer of your choice.

- **Hours of usage.** Make sure your reception venue can accommodate your guests for the time period you determine, rather than only between certain hours.

- **Ease of use.** Make sure that the venue you select offers everything you'll need for your reception, such as chairs, tables, china, flatware, barware, a place to cut the cake, dance space, electrical outlets, and so on.

- **Cost.** Your reception venue will likely be one of the costliest wedding-related items. Most venues charge a per-person cost, so your final head count will dictate the total bill.

- **Proximity to your ceremony location and accommodations.**
  While you don't want your guests to have to drive an hour between
  the ceremony and reception locations, a 10- to 30-minute drive is
  acceptable. If your reception isn't being held at a hotel or resort,
  make sure that hotel options are located near the reception venue
  for out-of-town guests.

Cost and Gratuity

If your reception venue will also cater the event, you'll likely pay one
fee for the facility rental and catering. However, if you use an outside
caterer, you'll pay separate bills for the facility rental and caterer. Because
most venues and caterers charge per person, your guest head count will
determine your final bill.

Make sure to read your contract to see exactly what's included and
to ensure that there will be no surprises. While some venues provide
essentials such as chairs, tables, china, flatware, glasses, barware, and
linens in their rental fee, other venues may offer these items à la carte—
or you may need to arrange to have them brought in yourself.

Most reception venues or caterers will also offer tiered food and
beverage/alcohol options that you can select, depending on your
preferences and budget. Options typically range from light or heavy hors
d'oeuvres and cocktails to buffet-style dinners or plated sit-down dinners
with an *open bar* or *cash bar*. Some couples also like to offer a cocktail
hour just before the reception, during which light refreshments can
also be served. Gratuity is typically included in most venue or caterers'
contracts. But if not, plan to have your best man deliver a tip that's 15 to
20 percent of your total bill.

Money-Saving Tips

If your reception budget is quickly going overboard, the first place to look is your guest list. Although it may be difficult to choose which people to cut from your list, eliminating some will ultimately reduce your costs. Consider making a compromise with your fiancée and cutting a few people (such as distant relatives or former co-workers) from both sides.

The next option is to look at your menu. Sometimes offering heavy hors d'oeuvres or a couple of entrées may be less expensive than providing a full buffet. Check with your venue or caterer to identify areas where you can minimize costs.

Another place to save money is alcohol. Instead of offering top-shelf liquors and mixed drinks, consider providing bottom-tier or house liquors or select just a couple alcoholic drinks to be served. Another option is a cash bar, where guests pay for their own alcoholic drinks or pay for drinks made with top-tier liquors. Keep in mind that this may turn off some guests, but if it means the difference between serving alcohol at your reception or none at all, this can be a safe choice.

Some venues may even let you purchase your own alcohol and bring it to the reception venue to save money. However, you'll most likely still have to pay for bar staff to mix and serve the alcoholic drinks. Also make sure to ask whether the venue charges a per-bottle cork fee to serve any wine you bring in, which will add to your cost.

The Rehearsal Dinner

The rehearsal dinner is arguably the largest responsibility for the groom and his family in the wedding-planning process. This event, which immediately follows the wedding rehearsal, is an opportunity to honor you and your bride one final time before you take you wedding vows. It also gives you a chance to thank your families and the wedding party for their support and for being such an important part of the wedding. While the wedding reception is the biggest party of the weekend, there's no reason why the rehearsal dinner can't hold its own.

If you're like most men, you probably don't have extensive event or party-planning experience. Rest assured, though, that throwing a memorable rehearsal dinner shouldn't be difficult for you and your family. Chances are that you've been to at least one rehearsal dinner in the past and can draw from that experience. Your parents may even want to incorporate some aspects of their own rehearsal dinner (location, menu, or photos) into yours.

Traditionally, you and your family are expected to arrange and pay for the rehearsal dinner. However, if you're unable to do so due to financial restrictions, it's perfectly acceptable for another family member or friend of the groom's family to take charge. This event doesn't need to be a ritzy, black-tie affair. While some couples like to stage a more formal event, others prefer to just invite the wedding party to their home for a backyard barbecue.

The Rehearsal

Before the rehearsal dinner fun can get started, everyone must show up at the ceremony venue for a run-through of the wedding ceremony. The rehearsal generally takes place on the day before the wedding. The following people will need to attend the wedding rehearsal:

- You and your bride
- Both sets of parents
- Important family members who will be part of the processional, such as grandparents
- The wedding party (groomsmen, bridesmaids, and ushers)
- Ancillary wedding party members, such as the ring bearer, flower girl, candle lighters, and readers

Traditionally, the rehearsal dinner guest list is comprised of the wedding party, immediate family, and anyone else who took part in the rehearsal. However, it's not uncommon to invite some out-of-town guests who have traveled for the wedding. This is another way to thank them for making the trip to be part of the big day. In those instances, it's not necessary for those guests to attend the rehearsal—although it's a nice gesture to extend the offer.

TRADITION SAYS
The groom and his family typically plan and pay for the rehearsal dinner. However, if the bride and her family have input, it's wise to let them weigh in. Work as a team, and you'll see great results.

This rehearsal serves as a practice round for the wedding ceremony. Your officiant leads the rehearsal and tells everyone when they need to show up on the following day. He or she also reminds everyone what their specific roles are. If everyone makes it to the rehearsal on time and pays attention, you can get this done in about an hour. And if you haven't yet decided where to seat important family members or which groomsmen should accompany each bridesmaid in the processional, this is the time to figure out those details. It's customary to have your ushers seat parents, siblings, and grandparents in the first two rows. This way, they have a front-row seat for all the action.

MAN DOWN
Don't be late for the wedding rehearsal. Because the rehearsal dinner will immediately follow, you'll be throwing off the night's entire schedule if you start the rehearsal late. Be sure to pass this information on to any habitually late groomsmen.

Rehearsal Dinner Planning Timeline

Before you begin planning the rehearsal dinner, it's a good idea to map out the timeline and set strategic goals to ensure a successful event. There's a lot to take note of, and you don't want to get overwhelmed. Here are a few important rehearsal dinner planning milestones you'll want to hit.

Nine to Twelve Months Out

- Locate and secure a venue. Determine the deposit amount and when the final balance is due.

- If you're using a caterer, book one as soon as possible—because the most popular are often booked more than a year in advance.

- Get a list of menu options from the venue or caterer. It's also helpful to ask for a list of the venue's and catering company's policies.

- Carefully review your caterer and venue contracts to make sure that everything fits your needs before signing on the dotted line.

Five to Six Months Out

- Decide on the specifics (menu options, open or cash bar, and so on), and sample the different types of food they offer.

- Begin preparing the guest list (complete with names and addresses).

- Select and order invitations (or make your own).

One to Two Months Out

- Address and send invitations.

- Keep detailed records of responses.

- Choose any special linens, flower arrangements, decorations, or any other touches you plan to use at the venue.

TRADITION SAYS
Unlike the wedding, you have a chance to be a little more casual and creative with the invitation style. If you're on a tight budget, electronic invites are a free alternative to the traditional invitation. Remember to wait to send the rehearsal dinner invites until after the wedding invitations have already gone out.

One Week Out

- Notify your caterer of the final head count, including how many children will attend.

- If applicable, draw a seating chart.

- Purchase name cards to place at tables for assigned seating.

Day-Of

- Visit the venue during the day to make sure everything is set up properly.

- Relax and enjoy the night!

- After the event, make sure that any personal belongings are removed from the venue. If you're required to do so, clean the area with help from friends and family members.

- Pay any outstanding balances to the caterer or venue.

Selecting a Venue and Caterer

When choosing a venue for your rehearsal dinner, the most important thing to remember is your head count. You need to make sure you have enough room for everyone. It's a safe bet that most, if not all, of your wedding party will be attending the rehearsal. Therefore, it should be easy to get a solid idea of the rehearsal dinner size. Ideally, the location of the venue should be relatively close to the ceremony location so there won't be a long delay for guests to get there after the rehearsal. Common venues include banquet halls, country clubs, restaurants, church halls, golf courses, hotel event space, and personal homes. Realistically, any venue with a suite or private room should be suitable.

For the groom, the rehearsal dinner is a chance to get creative. There are plenty of out-of-the-box venue options to choose. If you and your bride enjoy watching your favorite sports team together, see whether their stadium has any private suites available for rent (most do). Additionally, landmarks such as the Gateway Arch in St. Louis or Griffith Observatory in Los Angeles offer unique event spaces that will really wow your guests. Take a minute to think about the landmarks in your area, and consider looking into them for your rehearsal dinner.

MAN UP
Give the rehearsal dinner a different look and feel than the wedding reception. Make it your own by offering a totally unique menu, drink options, and décor than the wedding reception.

Unless you're holding the rehearsal dinner at a restaurant with menu options, you need to decide on a caterer and a menu. The main thing to remember is to make sure you don't duplicate the wedding reception menu. Here are some other things to keep in mind:

- Sample as much food as your caterer will allow. This is truly one of the best parts about wedding planning.

- Think about any dietary restrictions your guests may have. This may include vegetarians and vegans as well as people who have food allergies.

- Find out whether kids eat free. This is a standard practice with most caterers.

- Consider making a statement with the menu and adding a few personal favorites, such as hot wings or including a secret family recipe.

- Don't shell out money for an expensive dessert. Your groom's cake can be the ideal rehearsal dinner treat.

Another big decision is whether to have an open bar, cash bar, or no bar at all at the rehearsal dinner. Budget-wise, open bars can take a toll. One way to prevent breaking the bank is to serve only beer or wine, which will save you money compared to buying a large supply of liquor. However, if the budget is an issue, you don't have to offer alcohol at all. Everyone will get their fair share at the reception anyway.

If you're planning on serving booze at the rehearsal dinner, here are a few guidelines for stocking the bar:

- Make sure that your venue allows outside liquor. If they don't, get pricing on their house liquor and beer.

- Consider your head count when buying beer and soft drinks. You should plan on two beverages per person.

- Instead of buying multiple liquors and wines, consider having one or two signature cocktails for your guests to enjoy (perhaps you and your bride's two favorite drinks).

- When buying wine, include at least one white and one red. Another option is a white zinfandel, which is a lighter, fruitier option.

One Groom's Story
Chris in Kansas City

This is my favorite groom case study in this book because it's mine.
I was what most people would call a "hands-on" groom during our
wedding-planning months (just like I hope you'll be). When it came
time to discuss the rehearsal dinner, I indicated that I would like to
take over most of the planning responsibilities. While this event *is* traditionally a responsibility of the groom and his family, the bride and
her parents generally do have some input. However, I really wanted to
take the opportunity to shine and personalize the event to represent
me as the groom. Thanks to a great deal of trust on her part, my fiancée gave me the go-ahead to plan away.

Soon after our engagement, I dove headfirst into the planning. I was
set on leaving a personal mark on the event. To begin with, I already
knew that my dream venue was the private room at my favorite local
brew pub. The space featured an outdoor deck that overlooked down-
town, making it a prime location for weddings and special events.
I made sure to book the space as soon as I learned it was available,
because I knew the date wouldn't remain open for long. For food, the
decision was also easy. I had the event catered by my favorite local
barbecue joint. (What Midwestern guy doesn't love barbecue?) To top
things off, I designed custom invitations on my computer that high-
lighted the beer and barbecue theme of the evening. To call the event
"manly" would be accurate—but hey, I'm a guy!

The event was a hit because everyone in attendance appreciated the
effort I put into personalizing it, and it was a hell of a lot of fun for me
to do! I challenge all grooms to aim for the same.

Leaving a Personal Mark

You can make the rehearsal dinner memorable by making it more than just a dinner. Because it's a more intimate setting than the reception, it offers a great forum to get some of the customary wedding activities out of the way.

Speeches

Many couples opt to have all of the toasts or speeches take place at the rehearsal dinner. Getting these out of the way here allows for more time at the wedding reception for visiting and dancing. If you opt to go this route, be sure to give all your speakers a heads up so they have their words ready. You wouldn't want anyone getting up there and winging it, would you?

It's customary for the groom, fathers, the best man, and the maid-of-honor to give speeches honoring the newlyweds. However, it's always a nice gesture to offer the floor to anyone who might want to say a few words. Hey, it's not every day that you get toasted by the most important people in your life—so soak it up!

Video Montage

You've probably been to a wedding where a video montage of the bride and groom was shown. These montages include photos that document the lives of the newlyweds from childhood through the engagement. It's usually set to a playlist of you and your bride's favorite songs. Putting together this montage can be a joint effort between your family and the bride's. If you're making plans to put one together, the rehearsal dinner can be the perfect time to show it.

CHA-CHING

Are you and your family putting together a video montage for the wedding? You don't have to shell out mega bucks to get one made professionally. Most computers come with software that enables you to produce the montage on your own. Or, you can always recruit one of your tech-savvy friends to help.

Of course, you don't want to leave out your reception guests. While you can "premiere" the montage at the rehearsal dinner, you can also show it at the reception. I recommend playing it on a loop.

Handing Out Wedding Party Gifts

Many couples also use the rehearsal dinner to present gifts to their attendants and parents. When handing out gifts, be sure to introduce and say a few words about your best man, groomsmen, and ushers. You can tell a quick story about how you met each one or share a funny or meaningful experience that you went through together. Make it personal, and they'll truly appreciate it.

Cost- and Money-Saving Tips

Remember, the rehearsal dinner doesn't have to be a super-formal affair. In fact, sometimes the best ones aren't. If you're being extra mindful of the budget, consider hosting the rehearsal dinner as a backyard barbecue or even at a local park. This eliminates the need to secure a high-dollar venue. You might also check with your ceremony location to see whether they can provide a room for everyone to have dinner in immediately following the rehearsal.

MAN DOWN
If you're planning to host the rehearsal dinner at your home, be sure to let everyone know that it's entirely optional to bring a side dish or contribute to the food and drink offerings. They're already shelling out to be part of your wedding weekend, so you don't want to hang yet another obligation on them.

If you're going this route, there's no need to hire an expensive caterer, either. There are plenty of cost-effective outlets for food, such as grilling or cooking on your own, bringing in food from a favorite restaurant, or even having a pot-luck supper, where the groom and his family supply a few favorite dishes. Want to save even more coin? Cut liquor out of the equation to eliminate a huge chunk of the expenditures.

10

The Bachelor Party

I'd like to offer a warm welcome to the readers who skipped directly to this chapter. (You made an excellent choice.) As you've no doubt heard by now, the bachelor party is one of the best parties of your life because *you're* the guest of honor. To ensure an epic night (or weekend) of celebrating the end of your single status, you should think about a few simple things during the planning process.

Who Plans the Bachelor Party?

Tradition dictates that the best man is responsible for planning the groom's bachelor party (or "stag night"). His duties include inviting guests, making reservations, and building an itinerary worthy of your last night of freedom. If your best man lives out of town or has a hectic schedule, it's perfectly acceptable for him to share the planning responsibility with one or more groomsmen. It's also worth noting that there's a financial contribution involved in organizing a bachelor party. If your best man is capable, it's his duty to foot the bill for this night of debauchery.

However, bachelor party bills can often skyrocket depending on plans. Because of this, more and more bachelor parties are being planned by a committee these days, with other groomsmen, siblings, and dads chipping in. Going this route is a great way to split the costs and keep everyone's bank accounts in the black.

MAN DOWN
Don't hold your bachelor party a night or two before the wedding. You need to allow yourself ample recovery time unless you're prepared to deal with a fuming bride. The ideal time to hold the party is two to four weeks before the wedding day.

Who to Invite

Once you determine who's planning the party, you'll provide that person with a list of names, phone numbers, and e-mail addresses of your desired guests. It doesn't take a rocket scientist to determine this guest list. Brothers, groomsmen, and close friends are obvious shoo-ins. Male relatives, members of the bride's family, and co-workers may also warrant consideration.

It's also a nice gesture to include the fathers—both yours and your fiancée's. They'll definitely appreciate the invite. Just make sure to clarify whether they're invited only to dinner, or dinner and a couple drinks, or more. You may not want them around later in the night, depending on the itinerary. Although shot gunning beers may sound like a blast to you, it may not be your future father-in-law's idea of a good time.

Finally, if you have any younger siblings or other guests that aren't of age for bar-hopping or clubbing, it'll make their day if you schedule a portion of the party to include an all-ages event, such as a cookout, softball game, or trip to a sporting event. That way, everyone can take part in the festivities.

Things to Discuss Beforehand

If you haven't already thought about what kind of bachelor party you'd like to have, now's the time. Although traditional bachelor parties with strippers can be a blast, they can also lead to some time in the doghouse before the wedding. No matter how confident and trusting your fiancée is, there's always a little fear about what goes on at a strip club during a bachelor party. And although lying might seem like the easiest solution, it's best *not* to lie to her about your intentions. Trust me; these things always have a way of getting out eventually. Save yourself the fight later and 'fess up now.

It's also a good idea to discuss with at least one trustworthy friend what you are and aren't comfortable with beforehand. This is your party, so you should set the ground rules. It may be your quest to down 20 different shots, but make sure someone has your back on the off chance that your mission fails miserably and you need assistance. In my experience, it's also helpful to select a friend who happens to know the location of the nearest 24-hour tattoo-removal shop. You laugh now, but …

Traditional Bachelor Parties

It's no secret that bars and strip clubs have been long-time obligatory bachelor party haunts. If your ideal rite of passage involves drinks and drunken debauchery, here are a few things to keep in mind:

- Some bars won't allow bachelor party groups in the door. Make sure your best man confirms that your destination will accommodate the size of your group.

- Always make sure someone has plenty of cash on hand for unexpected—yet often inevitable—expenses, such as tips, extra cab fares, hospital co-pays, bail money, and so on.

- Whether you're heading to a strip club or having the talent come to you, make sure everyone in the group is aware of policy and proper behavior. Strippers won't perform if they sense trouble. And you're likely to be booted from the club if a bouncer deems you too drunk or rowdy.

- Strippers expect generous tips during and after their performances. Make sure your crew has plenty of bills if they want a good show, and *never*—under any circumstances—ask a stripper for change!

Beyond Booze and Poles

Not into binge drinking? Looking for something beyond the standard fare? There are plenty of options for the more adventurous groom. Adventure or "extreme" bachelor parties have been gaining popularity as grooms and best men try to plan memorable, less-traditional parties. These are bachelor parties held in a destination other than a bar or strip club. Popular activities include golfing, camping, and paintballing.

MAN UP
If some of your friends aren't big partiers, it's a nice gesture to plan a bachelor party that includes activities they can get excited about as well, such as golfing or attending a pro ballgame.

Inform your best man in advance if he'll be arranging this type of party, because the planning will likely involve extra research time. These types of outings can either take place in your hometown or on a planned out-of-town weekend excursion. Need some ideas? Here are a few beyond-traditional bachelor parties to consider.

For the Golfer

A golf outing can be fun for including the dads, uncles, and any other older relatives. Be sure to let the best man know a couple of your favorite local golf courses and approximate player head count so he can set up tee times in advance. If your players have a wide range of skill levels, consider playing scramble-style (best ball) to help level the playing field.

If you're feeling more ambitious, perhaps road-tripping to play a famous course would be appropriate. Pebble Beach (California), Pinehurst (North Carolina), Shadow Creek (Nevada), TPC Sawgrass (Florida), and the Robert Trent Jones Golf Trail (Alabama) are all public courses that offer serious challenges for even the most skilled golfers.

For the Outdoorsman

If you're an avid outdoorsman, chartering a fishing boat or renting a cabin in the mountains can be a lot of fun. It's a no-brainer for grooms who love skiing, fishing, or hunting. Even if all the guys aren't outdoorsmen, most people can quickly learn the basics and still have a great time.

You may not think you live in an area that's conducive to these types of destinations, but I bet you'd be surprised. Ski resorts are common near most large cities. For fishing and hunting, Lake Lanier (Georgia), Lake of the Ozarks (Missouri), Indian Lake (Tennessee), and any of the great lakes are perfect for you and your boys to get in touch with nature.

For the Extreme Sports Enthusiast

Skydiving, bungee jumping, or a NASCAR driving experience are all excellent options for adrenaline junkies who enjoy pushing the limits of sanity. Of course, if you want to try something a little less heart-attack inducing, there's always paintball or rock climbing.

Some of these outings require advance deposits or reservations. Make sure your best man is aware of this and has the details and money lined up beforehand so you don't show up and learn that the place is booked for the day.

For the Card Shark

Are you known by name at the local poker and blackjack tables? Reserving a hotel room at a casino allows the group to gamble, eat, and drink all evening. The bonus is having a place to stay at the end of a long night of partying.

If some of your party guests are underage, organize a casino night at someone's house. This more intimate setting allows for house rules and smaller betting. This way, everyone doesn't run out of money after 15 minutes.

Vegas Bachelor Parties

If you're the one guy in America who hasn't seen *The Hangover,* go bury your head in shame. It's no secret that Sin City has long been a favorite bachelor party destination. For a guy spending his final days as a single man, the city simply has it all.

However, as we learned from the movie, some guys just can't handle Vegas. If you decide to embark on this journey, make sure that each member of your wolf pack is up for the challenge. Prerequisites include the ability to stay upright for long periods of time without sleep; having enough cash to withstand a weekend of gambling, dining, and tipping; and being cool with strippers.

Here are five important tips based on my own experiences at Vegas bachelor parties:

- It's worth the extra money to get your own bed or room.

- Get an extra room key and have one on you at all times.

- Bring your own soap and towels. If you've ever shared a hotel room with a group of guys, you know why.

- Leave your ATM card in your hotel room.

- Keep yourself hydrated.

Co-Ed Bachelor(ette) Parties

It may sound odd, but *co-ed bachelor(ette) parties* are actually increasing in popularity as couples who have overlapping circles of friends look for ways to party as a group before the wedding. The groom and bride usually take charge of planning this outing. The challenge is finding a destination that both sexes can get excited about. One idea is a group wine-tasting trip. Assuming you reside in an area rich with vineyards, this option can make for a fine co-ed party. This may come as a surprise, but you don't have to live in California to be near "wine country." Washington, Oregon, and other states such as Missouri, New York, and Michigan are churning out some of the country's best-tasting wines. Here are a few tips for planning this outing:

- Find an area with multiple wineries, and call ahead to make sure your choices can accommodate larger groups.

- This type of trip can get pricy, so ask everyone to chip in a few bucks to lessen the burden.

- Rent a bus or trolley that can take everyone from stop to stop. This important step will ensure that everyone can enjoy drinking without worrying about a designated driver.

- Plan lunch and dinner stops along the way. The last thing you want is for half the group to pass out after the second stop. (Then again, if they can't keep up, why are you friends with them anyway?)

- If it's an overnight trip, book a hotel well in advance. If you're planning to go home afterward, arrange safe transportation for everyone.

If this sounds like a fun idea but you're not into wine, try a brewery tour, liquor tasting, or local restaurant tour instead.

MAN UP

The Groom's Toast is a popular (and aptly named) bachelor party concoction that consists of three shots of whiskey, three full beers, and a can of frozen lemonade. Mixed and served in a pitcher, this baby is ideal for pre-gaming before hitting the bars.

Wrapping Things Up

Gifts aren't necessary, but thanking your guests at some point during the outing with a toast, shot, or after-dinner drink is a nice gesture.

Finally, I know I've mentioned this before, but make sure to party responsibly with your gang on the big night. You're no good as a groom if you're in jail—or worse—and the same goes for your guests. Make sure you have ample transportation options to make this a party everyone survives to reminisce about in the future.

11

Wedding Showers

I know what you're thinking: wedding showers are for chicks, right? Although that may have traditionally been the case, times are definitely changing. In addition to the typical bridal showers your fiancée will attend with her female friends and family, today's wedding showers often incorporate both men and women—and some even focus solely on guys.

Do I Have to Take Part?

The short answer is yes. But before you go jumping off the nearest bridge, keep in mind that it isn't the nightmare you're imagining. Co-ed showers can actually be fun. Take it from a guy who has been there and survived to tell the tale—and even enjoyed himself.

Best of all, attending a wedding shower means going home with loot— and lots of it. This is the groom's opportunity to be "showered" with gifts he can get excited about, too (think power tools, tech gadgets, and bar and grill accessories).

Man Showers: It's Not What It Sounds Like

Although the name may cause some confusion, a *man shower* is basically a bridal shower on steroids. It's an excuse to get the guys together for some hang time (such as grilling out and drinking, most likely while watching sports) before the groom officially wifes up. The main rule is to make it a men-only event. After all, your fiancée will have plenty of ladies-only showers. Why shouldn't guys have one of their own?

The man shower is often held during the day—typically before the bachelor party, either at the home of your best man, a groomsman, a relative, or at an outside location such as a pro ballgame, golf outing, or brewery tour. Consider inviting your best guy friends, including those in your wedding party as well as any close family members, such as siblings and cousins and your dad and future father-in-law.

 MAN UP
Don't forget to include your dad and future father-in-law in a couple of manly pre-wedding events, such as a man shower, so you can spend some time together before the wedding and make them feel included in the process. They're probably covering some—if not all—of the wedding costs, so make sure to show them your appreciation with an invitation to celebrate with the guys.

One key item to include in any man shower is food. To please most men's palates, you can't go wrong with grilled or fried foods. If you have a deep fryer on hand, the possibilities are virtually endless. Some excellent fried-food choices include chicken wings, fish, pickles, and peppers. For grilling, you can go with the traditional burgers, dogs, brats, chicken, steak, or fish, or try kicking things up a notch by grilling something a little different, such as spicy lamb sliders. To enhance the flavor, try grilling meat on cedar planks.

Want to go beyond the backyard cookout and really class things up? Try a liquor-, wine-, or beer-tasting party. If your boys are Scotch drinkers, you can't go wrong with the "Keep on Walking, Johnnie" shower theme. In a nutshell: the hosting group of guys goes in together to purchase five bottles of Johnnie Walker Scotch, one of each blend available (in order from the least to most expensive: Red Label, Black Label, Green Label, Gold Label, and the famously coveted Blue Label). Before the party begins, a host disguises the bottles so that no one knows which blend is inside and randomly assigns a number to each bottle. Once guests have arrived, a host pours Scotch into shot glasses or highballs (no plastic cups here). As guests begin tasting, they list each drink from one to five in order of their most favorite to least favorite. Once all of the blends have been sampled, the bottles are uncovered to reveal which guests have the most distinguished palates by identifying the blends in the correct order.

If your bros aren't into Scotch, sample low-, mid-, or higher-priced bottles of your liquor of choice; taste wines of a single variety; or sample a range of artisan beers to identify everyone's favorites. As always, when alcohol is involved, make sure to pair your drinks with plenty of food and ensure that everyone drinks responsibly or takes a cab home.

Looking for another fun idea that doesn't focus on alcohol? Try a groom's roast. Friends of the groom gather to talk trash and dish dirt on the groom's notorious single past. To make it authentic, have everyone dress up for the occasion (à la the Rat Pack), complete with martinis and cigars in hand if you like, and use a lectern with long tables flanking either side with space for "audience" (or guest) seating in front. Of course, because raunchy humor is encouraged and expected here, this type of event works best with brothers and close friends.

Finally, while gifts are never required, don't forget to register for some manly gifts beforehand to give your pals a heads-up on what kinds of gifts you could use, if they feel so inclined (see Chapter 5 for ideas on some must-have gifts to include on every groom's registry). Remember, your fiancée will receive loads of girly gifts at her shower(s), so don't miss this chance to score some gifts you'd like as well—whether it's for the bar, grill, man cave, game room, lawn, or tool shed.

Couples Showers

Say what? That's right, a phenomenon known as the *couples shower* has become very popular in recent years. Both men and women attend these wedding showers, which feature themes and gifts that appeal to both sexes. While a female-oriented bridal shower might have a "kitchen and bath" theme, for example, a couples shower typically has a theme that both the bride and groom can enjoy, such as "bar and grill."

Shower Themes

If someone offers to throw you a couples shower, they might ask if you'd like to go with a particular theme. This is a perfect opportunity to get creative and consider something that's meaningful to you as a couple. (These are also great ideas to consider if you need to throw a shower for someone else in the future.) The following sections include a few ideas to spark your creativity.

Bar-and-Grill Shower

Whether the engaged couple already has a bar or grill at home or simply enjoys entertaining guests, a bar-and-grill shower is a great way to include the groom and other guys in the pre-wedding festivities. This is a perfect shower for groomsmen or friends of the groom to organize. Gift ideas include barware, bar utensils and accessories, bottles of liquor, grilling accessories, or even a group gift of a new grill if the couple doesn't already have one or theirs has seen better days.

As with all themed showers, when creating the invitations, make sure to include the shower's theme on the invitation so guests will know what types of gifts to bring. Also, make sure the couple has already registered for a few theme-appropriate items for guests to consider.

This shower's guest list easily lends itself to the wedding party and friends of the couple but can also include close family members and extended relatives. Bar-and-grill showers are often held during evening hours and can either offer drinks and hors d'oeuvres or even a full meal—cooked on the grill, of course.

MAN UP
Need a macho cocktail to serve at your man or couples shower? You can't beat the Manhattan. This man-tastic drink blends whiskey, sweet vermouth, and bitters. Stir with ice, strain into a lowball glass, and serve on the rocks. To enhance the flavor, add muddled maraschino cherries.

Lawn-and-Garden Shower

If the engaged couple has a yard, you can bet they'll need equipment to keep it looking its best as well as to outfit it for entertaining guests. This shower works well as an afternoon or evening backyard barbecue or cocktail party. Gift options include yard-preening basics such as lawn-cutting, landscaping, and gardening tools and equipment as well as entertaining and recreational essentials such as outdoor furniture, fire pits, chimineas, tiki torches, hammocks, and backyard games such as putting greens, horseshoes, washers, croquet, or badminton.

Home-Improvement Shower

Whether the engaged couple lives in a home, apartment, or condo, their humble abode will require several tools and gadgets to assist in countless repair and upgrade projects in the years to come. Besides, what groom doesn't need to gear up for the impending "honey-do" list ("Honey, could you mow the lawn, clean the gutters, stain the deck …?")? Groomsmen or friends of the couple can throw a home-improvement shower to equip the newlyweds with everything they need to keep their home in tip-top shape, such as ladders, tool sets or a new tool bench, painting equipment, or hardware store gift cards.

Or, consider hosting a working shower where guests help the couple paint or make over a room in their home. Ask guests to bring new tools and other items to aid in the task or roll up their sleeves and give the gift of free labor in exchange for dinner and drinks while basking in the glow of a job well done.

Honeymoon Shower

If the couple has a honeymoon location picked out ahead of time, the wedding party or friends of the couple can host a honeymoon shower, where guests bring gifts that can either be put toward or used on the honeymoon. Depending on the destination, gifts could include excursions and activities (such as jet-ski rides, moped tours, or helicopter rides), snorkeling gear, hiking equipment, beach towels, luggage, or travel guides.

If the couple is planning to honeymoon in a tropical or beach locale, have guests dress in Hawaiian shirts and luau gear and serve food or cocktails inspired by their destination to create a festive mood. If the couple hasn't yet decided on a destination or plans to save up for a honeymoon at a later date, have guests bring cash gifts that can be put toward future honeymoon plans. Another cool idea: create invitations that look like passports or plane tickets.

12

The Honeymoon

Ah, the honeymoon. Post-wedding is excellent timing for a vacation. A getaway and a little alone time together is just what the doctor ordered for you and the new Mrs. after months of tireless wedding planning, in addition to a physically and emotionally (yep, I said it) exhausting wedding day. The honeymoon is the perfect time to relax and recharge your batteries before you start your new life together as husband and wife.

Whether you plan to honeymoon at a resort, hotel, bed-and-breakfast, or on a cruise ship, this is your time to shine, guys. The groom is usually in charge of planning the honeymoon. According to tradition, the groom and his family also typically cover the cost of the trip—although today, the couple may pay for the honeymoon together. Or, both sets of parents, other relatives, and friends may chip in as well.

Timing

The majority of newlyweds choose to go on a honeymoon within a week after the wedding, with most leaving the day after or even the night of the wedding. However, the reality of crazy work schedules and depleted finances can easily come into play here.

There's no shame in putting off your honeymoon plans until you both can take some time off work or when you can better afford it. Another option for cash-strapped couples is to take a "mini-moon" or a shorter, less-expensive weekend trip now until you can save up for a longer, more expensive trip down the line.

The bottom line: take your honeymoon whenever it makes most sense for you and your bride. There's no sense in putting extra strain on your finances to go right after the wedding if you can put it off for a while. Starting off your marriage in debt to cover your honeymoon definitely isn't worth it.

TRADITION SAYS
The groom and his family have traditionally covered the cost of the honeymoon. However, today couples may pay for the honeymoon together—or both sets of parents may help the couple foot the bill or even cover its costs as a wedding gift.

Travel Options

Like most vacations, endless possibilities are available when it comes to arranging your honeymoon plans. You'll likely only be limited by your budget, time frame, and passport status (if you plan to travel out of the country—more on that later).

If you're not quite sure what type of honeymoon trip is right for you, start by asking yourself and your bride-to-be these questions:

- When you think of your ideal vacation, is it in a warmer or cooler destination?

- Do you like exploring new places?

- Are you afraid of flying or feel claustrophobic on cruise ships?

- When it comes to vacation length, do you prefer shorter trips over longer ones?

- Do you prefer vacationing in destinations that cater to adult couples or are more family-friendly?

- Are you willing to travel on a very long flight to get to a hard-to-reach destination?

- Do you prefer to stay in one place or visit several nearby destinations in a single trip?

- Are you more comfortable staying in accommodations that offer various on-site dining and entertainment options, or do you prefer venturing outside for these activities?

- Do you mind visiting a destination that's very popular with other tourists, or do you prefer a locale that's more off-the-beaten-path?

- Do you prefer active and adventurous or leisurely and relaxing vacations?

- Are you open to traveling to places where English isn't the primary language?

- Are you interested in learning about new cultures and trying new cuisines?

- Do you like staying mainly indoors or enjoying the outdoors on vacation?

- Is it important to you to choose a destination with an active nightlife?

Answering these questions honestly should help you narrow down your travel options and choose your ideal honeymoon location.

Trip Types

Once you've decided how long you can be away and what kind of trip appeals to you, take some time to consider the options covered in the following sections.

Cruises

Although each cruise line is different and may focus on different features and services, cruises generally include accommodations and all meals as well as some beverages, such as water and juice. Cruises allow guests to visit many different ports-of-call in a single trip. Beyond the standard pools, restaurants, and bars, many ships also offer more unique features, such as ice-skating rinks, movie theaters, rock-climbing walls, and surf parks. Cruises also typically offer a variety of on-board dining and entertainment options for both singles and families.

What you'll love:

- Most cruises provide the luxury of being able to visit several different countries or islands while unpacking only once.

- If you love to eat and sample a variety of different cuisines on your trip, cruises typically offer a wide range of both casual and fine dining options onboard.

- If you enjoy a variety of entertainment choices, such as karaoke night, Broadway-type shows, piano bars, diving contests, dance-offs, and more, cruises typically offer it all.

- Cruises can be less expensive than staying in a regular hotel and venturing out on your own for meals and entertainment.

- Some cruises cater specifically to adult couples if you prefer a more romantic atmosphere.

What to consider:

- Soft drinks and alcoholic beverages are almost always extra.

- You'll likely have to wait in longer lines (unless you choose a smaller ship) and participate in a few mandatory activities, such as a muster/emergency drill and lengthy embarking and disembarking processes.

- While some cruises offer private dining for couples, others may assign you to a larger table with other guests for dining. Likewise, some cruises allow you to eat whenever you like, while others only offer set meal times. Cruises may also set dress codes for certain evenings or restaurants. Make sure to research your cruise line's policies ahead of time.

- If motion sickness affects you or your wife, you may need to enlist over-the-counter remedies (such as medication, patches, or armbands) to ward it off. Usually, one of these options does the trick. Of course, if you're prone to severe motion sickness, you may want to avoid cruises altogether.

MAN UP
Love to tie one on but hate paying for outrageous bar tabs on vacation? Consider an all-inclusive trip where all-you-can-drink alcoholic beverages are included in the cost. No need to tip the bartender, either—gratuity is also included. Cheers!

All-Inclusives

As the name suggests, all-inclusive hotels, resorts, and cruises charge a flat, per-person rate for your accommodations, food and beverages (both alcoholic and non-alcoholic), snacks, and even some services and activities (such as golf, cabanas by the beach, or the use of sports equipment and other amenities). Some all-inclusives also throw in basic wedding packages if you're planning a destination wedding.

What you'll love:

- With all-inclusives, you'll only pay once for your trip, without having to reach for your wallet every time you want to grab a drink or a bite to eat. Gratuity is also included.

- Alcoholic beverages are included. As most of us know all too well, the cost of alcoholic drinks can really add up on a trip, so including them up front can save you money.

- Some activities and services are also included. On another trip, you'd pay extra for activities such as bicycle rental, snorkeling gear, and golfing, which are often included here.

- All-inclusives can also be less expensive than staying in a standard hotel and seeking out your own meals and entertainment.

- Some all-inclusives cater to adult couples.

What to consider:

- If you're not a drinker, you may feel like you're paying for alcoholic drinks you won't be consuming. (Although, you may be able to take advantage of other free options instead.)

- If you prefer to venture outside the property often for meals, you may prefer not to pre-pay for on-site meals through the all-inclusive.

Hotels and Resorts

Many high-end and luxury hotels and resorts are available in nearly every destination imaginable. Some offer amenities such as full-service spas, pools, hot tubs, on-site fine-dining options, fitness centers, and much more.

What you'll love:

- The freedom to come and go as you please.

- The ability to create your own itinerary as you see fit. Want to stay in bed or lounge by the pool all day? No problem. Want to venture out for dinner and a show? Go for it. It's all up to you.

- Honeymoon or couples packages, which include extras such as private dining, massages, shopping, and show tickets, are often available at a discounted rate.

What to consider:

- Meals, drinks, spa services, and other activities are extra unless you book a specific package.

- Unless your hotel offers the on-site restaurants and services you're interested in, you'll have to venture elsewhere (and likely also pay for transportation) to find them.

Popular Destinations

Once you've decided what kind of honeymoon you'd like to take, it's time to find a destination that best fits the bill. If you haven't had a chance to investigate the endless options available yet, here are some popular honeymoon destinations to consider.

Tropical:

- Hawaii
- U.S. Virgin Islands (St. Croix, St. John's, and St. Thomas)
- Mexico
- Bahamas
- Jamaica
- St. Lucia
- Aruba
- Antigua
- Cayman Islands
- Barbados
- St. Barts
- St. Maarten
- Turks and Caicos
- Tahiti

Domestic:

- Florida
- California
- Las Vegas
- New York City
- North or South Carolina
- Massachusetts

- Arizona
- Colorado

European:

- France
- Italy
- United Kingdom
- Greece
- Belgium
- Germany
- Spain

Asian:

- Japan
- China
- Hong Kong
- Thailand

South American:

- Brazil
- Argentina
- Peru
- Chile

Other options:

- Australia
- New Zealand
- Africa
- Egypt
- Canada

MAN DOWN

Don't book a trip to a particular country or region without first checking the websites of the U.S. State Department (www.travel. state.gov) or the Transportation Security Administration (www.tsa. gov) to see whether any travel warnings or alerts have been issued for your destination. Even if there hasn't been a major political uprising in your destination recently, there may be other issues (such as recent terrorism or natural disaster threats) that could affect travelers. Don't be cavalier about your safety.

When to Book

As they say, there's no time like the present. As with most other travel arrangements, this is especially true for your honeymoon plans. If you're planning to honeymoon in a popular domestic destination, in another country, or on a cruise, you should book your trip as soon as possible— or at a minimum of six months out. Not only will booking in advance help ensure availability, but it will also most likely help reduce your overall costs. Prices on flights and hotels almost always increase if you wait to book them at the last minute.

Even if you're only planning to take a trip to another state, you should book your flight and hotel as early as possible. Trust me—you won't want to deal with your bride if you end up without a place to stay on the first night of your honeymoon.

Booking in Her Maiden Name

If your fiancée is planning to take your last name after you're married, she's likely already thinking about herself with her new last name (especially with all of the monogramming related to your wedding). However, when booking your honeymoon travel plans, make sure to book them in her maiden name rather than her married name. You'd be surprised at how many couples forget to do this.

You won't be able to legally change her last name until after the wedding, and it will likely take several weeks to do so (for more details on that, see Chapter 16). Make sure to save yourself the honeymoon-ruining headache at the airport by booking her tickets in her maiden name so they'll match her current driver's license or passport.

Budgeting Tips

If you're planning to cover the honeymoon yourself or will be saving up for it with your bride, it's important to start setting money aside for it as early as possible. If you wait until all the other wedding expenses have been covered, unexpected budget overages may end up draining your honeymoon fund before you get to it. It pays to start budgeting for it up front.

If you know you definitely won't be able to cover the cost of a honeymoon on your own, consider setting up a honeymoon registry online so your wedding guests can help fund your post-wedding vacay (see

Chapter 5 for more information on setting up a honeymoon registry). If you and your bride already have many of the typical household necessities that guests would give you as wedding presents, having them cover the honeymoon, excursions, or spending money can be a great alternative. Make sure to let guests know about your plans through your wedding website or via word of mouth.

When setting your budget, don't forget about all the associated costs, such as air, train, bus, or cruise fare; accommodations; rental cars; airport shuttles; cab fare; food and drinks; excursions or activities (such as couples massages, private beach-side dinners, helicopter tours, and so on); passport renewal (if applicable); spending money for shopping and souvenirs; and travel insurance.

MAN UP
Make sure to mention that you're on your honeymoon when you check in for your flight at the airport as well as board your cruise ship or check in to your hotel. This is one time when it pays to brag a bit. If you keep quiet, you could be missing out on free upgrades and other perks. Many airlines and hotels will offer you comped upgrades and services if you tell them you're traveling on your honeymoon. Another good move is mentioning that this is your dream vacation and how excited you are about it.

When you're ready to book your trip, make sure to mention that it will be your honeymoon. Many airlines, hotel, and cruise accommodations offer free or discounted upgrades and other perks (such as champagne and chocolates in your room upon arrival, free massages, or other activities).

How Much Money to Bring

The prevalence of ATM machines, which easily allow you to obtain foreign currency in other countries, and the wider acceptance of

American credit cards in many travel destinations have made traveling much easier for Americans today. In fact, most often, simply arming yourself with a little cash (for cab fare, tipping, and incidentals), an ATM card, and a major credit card or two is sufficient for most trips. Of course, traveler's checks are another safe option if you feel more comfortable using them.

So how much cash should you bring on your honeymoon? Depending on your destination, you should typically plan to take about $200 to $300 cash (or $100 for each of you) on any trip. If you need more cash later on, you'll likely be able to hit up an ATM. Even in most major cities in foreign countries, swiping your American ATM card will quickly provide you with the destination's equivalent currency. However, if you know you'll be visiting a much more remote area with less access to ATMs, you should plan to bring more cash to exchange into the area's currency upon your arrival.

To dodge the highest fees, avoid exchanging currency at the airport whenever possible, unless you're using an ATM. Instead, seek out a bank beyond the airport. However, if you're in a destination that's new to you and safety is a concern, paying the extra fees—and taking advantage of the convenience—at the airport might be worth it.

American credit cards such as MasterCard, Visa, and American Express are accepted in most foreign destinations. However, if you're not 100 percent sure about your preferred credit card's acceptability, check with your carrier beforehand to see whether your destination typically accepts it.

If you don't frequently travel (especially outside the United States), it's also a good idea to inform your credit card company or bank about your trip a few days or weeks beforehand so they don't interpret the wave of larger purchases abroad as fraudulent activity and shut off your card. (You'll also avoid figuring out how to make an international call back to your U.S.-based carrier to reactivate it.) Nothing can put a damper on a trip quicker than having your credit card shut off after the first day.

Excursions and Activities

Before booking extra activities (or excursions, as they're called on cruise ships), such as deep-sea fishing, helicopter tours, surfing lessons, dolphin watching, mountain climbing, and so on, from the first random vendor who approaches you on the beach or once you set foot outside the hotel, do some homework. The safest bet is to check with your hotel, resort, or cruise concièrge for a list of recommended activity vendors. Often, the concièrge or tour director can even book the activity, as well as transportation to and from it, for you—saving you the extra time and hassle.

While the resort or cruise's recommended options may not be the least-expensive ones available, you can rest assured that the vendors will have your safety in mind and that the companies won't take your money and run. To save money, you can always surf for deals online, but make sure that the vendor you choose is licensed and insured at a minimum. Another good bet? See whether the company is recommended by the state or country's tourism bureau or other respected industry association. Remember: the best deal isn't always the best (or safest) option.

Tipping

Tipping practices can vary widely depending on your honeymoon destination. Although you should always check into the tipping policy associated with your travel plans, here's a typical rule of thumb for some popular honeymoon options:

- **Cruises:** most cruise lines tack on a daily gratuity rate to your bill, which is split up between each of the staff members serving you during your trip. If you feel that individual staff members did an exceptional job, you can tip more. However, if you feel that a particular staff member's service was sorely lacking, speak to your concièrge to reduce the gratuity applied to that portion of your stay.

- **All-inclusives:** as the name suggests, gratuity should be included in most all-inclusive resorts, although you can tip individual members extra if you feel they went above and beyond your expectations.

- **Overseas countries:** in general, most foreign countries (such as those in Europe and Asia) add gratuity to your bill, so additional tipping isn't required unless you feel the staff's service was exceptional.

Planning Tips

As the saying goes, hindsight is always $^{20}/_{20}$. Here are a few travel-planning tips that some couples wish they had considered before booking their honeymoons:

- If you're planning to travel to a tropical or island destination, consider the typical hurricane season for the area.

- Consider all-inclusive options. Located in many destinations, all-inclusive resorts offer accommodations, food and beverages, services, and some activities for one flat rate. Staying within the confines of these resorts can also often be a safer and more secure alternative to venturing out to nearby areas of your destination city or country.

- Saving up a small fortune for your dream honeymoon? Consider purchasing travel insurance in case a natural disaster (such as an earthquake, volcano eruption, or tsunami) or medical emergency ends up ruining or postponing your plans.

- When reserving a hotel room in a foreign destination, such as Europe, make sure to book an en-suite room, which includes an attached bathroom. Otherwise, you may be sharing a communal bathroom with all the other guests on your floor (not so romantic).

- Call ahead to ask whether your airline carrier, cruise ship, or hotel offers free or discounted room/seat upgrades or other perks because it's your honeymoon trip.

- Really wow your wife by having them stock your room with champagne, strawberries, and rose petals upon your arrival. (Again, these items may even be comped if you mention it's your honeymoon or book a special honeymoon package.)

- Talk to friends, relatives, or acquaintances who have visited your destination to get insider advice and tips on what to skip and what not to miss. Don't know anyone who has been there? Research online travel sites and forums to see what other travelers recommend.

- Ask your hotel, resort, or cruise concièrge for advice when dining offsite or arranging excursions or activities to avoid disappointment and getting duped by local scammers.

- Consider a destination wedding to combine your wedding and honeymoon locations and potentially reduce overall costs.

Passport or Visa Required?

If you're planning to visit a destination that requires a passport, now's the time to start thinking about it. If you already have a valid passport ... somewhere ... locate it and check the expiration date (U.S. passports are valid for 10 years from their issue date). If it will still be valid by the time your trip rolls around, put it in a secure place (maybe in the suitcase you'll be taking) until then, so it doesn't get lost.

If your passport is already expired or will expire before or during your trip, you'll need to renew it. Likewise, if you and/or your bride don't already have passports, now's the time to apply for them. Wait times for passport application and renewal processing can often be lengthy, so it's wise to start the process as soon as possible or at a minimum of three months prior to your trip.

MAN DOWN
Need a passport for your honeymoon trip? Don't wait until the last minute. Passport processing can often take weeks or months, depending on the current backlog, so make sure to apply for yours as soon as possible. Blew it anyway? Check into expedited service, which may get your new passport to you in time—for an extra charge, of course.

Check the State Department's website (www.travel.state.gov) for passport information, such as instructions on renewals and first-time applications, forms, ID and photo requirements, fees, and passport office locations as well as expected wait times for routine and expedited services. (Yes, expedited services are available at an additional charge if you're in a rush.)

Some foreign countries also require travelers to have a valid visa for entry. While some visas can be obtained online with a credit card, others require more paperwork and a lengthier application process. Research your destination's visa requirements, and apply for them ahead of time as well.

Keeping Your Rings Safe

We've all heard horror stories of brides who managed to lose their engagement and/or wedding ring or have them stolen during their honeymoon. Whether she lost it while swimming in the ocean, at the hotel spa, or maybe even had it mysteriously disappear from the hotel room, it can be a trip-ruining experience. You've made a major investment in her ring, and it's important to do whatever you can to protect it.

Of course, you already have ring insurance in case something does happen to the ring. But another great solution is to buy a fake ring just for the honeymoon or other future travels. Rings made of cubic zirconia, moissanite, or other stones can be excellent substitutes. Some jewelers even offer exact replicas of the ring you purchased. Going this route can give you piece of mind as well as make her feel like less of a target while traveling.

Another option? If your bride's willing, she can opt to wear only her wedding band on your honeymoon and keep her larger engagement ring safe at home. That way, she'll be protecting her more-important investment but will still be wearing a wedding ring on your trip.

Likewise, guys, you'll also need to keep an eye on your wedding band during the honeymoon. Although your ring probably didn't cost quite as much as your wife's, you don't want to lose it as soon as you get it. You'd be surprised at how many guys end up losing their wedding rings on their honeymoons. Unlike women, most men aren't used to wearing rings and aren't as apt to notice if it happens to slip off while swimming or changing. Make sure to be aware of your ring at all times to keep it safe. You'll get used to it eventually, and it will become part of you. But until then, look down every now and again to make sure it's still on your meaty finger.

Honeymoon Packing Checklist

With the wedding just around the corner, it's important to start packing for your honeymoon a few days ahead of time so you don't end up rushing to toss a suitcase together the night before (or worse, the day of). The last thing you want to worry about is forgetting to pack something essential for your honeymoon trip.

A word of advice: to avoid extra baggage-checking fees, try to limit yourself to one overhead-size suitcase and one carry-on bag (such as a duffle, backpack, or computer bag) per person. (Trust me: if my wife and I can take two-week trips to Asia, Europe, and Australia without having to check a single bag, so can you.)

Because you also won't be able to check liquids or gels, you'll need to pack a quart-size zipper-top bag with any liquid essentials, such as travel-size (3 oz. or less) toothpaste, sunscreen, shampoo, conditioner, face wash, body wash, hair gel, and antibacterial hand gel. (And yes, my wife can fit all of her makeup essentials in her plastic bag as well and take advantage of the extra space in mine for any overrun.)

Here's a quick checklist of essential items to pack:

- Shoes. For nearly every trip, you'll need one pair of tennis shoes, nice dress shoes, and flip-flops or sandals (even if you're going to a cool destination, it's nice to have flip-flops to wear around your hotel room or down to the hot tub).

- Socks, both casual and dress.

- Underwear. Don't forget your skivvies!

- Shorts, jeans, and khakis or dress pants. Even if you're going some-place warm, pack at least one pair of long pants for nice dinners.

- Undershirts, T-shirts, and button-down shirts (casual and dress).

- A sport coat, light jacket, or hooded sweatshirt. Even in a tropical locale, it can sometimes get chilly at night during long walks on the beach. If you have a light rain jacket, pack it, too.

- Pajamas, if you're not a "sleeps commando" kind of guy.

- Mangerie (that's male lingerie, such as silk boxers or snazzy bikini briefs to impress your new bride).

- Lingerie, if you're planning to give this to your wife as a wedding gift.

- A hat or baseball cap to shield you from wind, rain, or the sun.

- Sunglasses. Also toss in a case so they don't get scratched or smashed when you stash them in your carry-on.

- Eyeglasses and/or contact lenses, case, and solution.

- A swimsuit. Even if you're not headed to a warm locale, pack your suit in case you want to hit the hotel pool or hot tub.

- Any prescription or over-the-counter medication you may need.

- A toothbrush and dental floss.

- A comb or hair brush.

- A straight or electric razor (make sure it's fully charged before you leave).

- Passport (and visa, if necessary) and driver's license.

- Your wallet, cash, and credit cards.

- Your cell phone and charger. Also bring an outlet converter if you're traveling to a foreign country.

- Camera, video camera, and extra batteries for each to capture honeymoon memories.

- iPod or MP3 player, plus a car adapter if you'll be using it in a rental car.

- Laptop computer, if necessary. If at all possible, leave it at home. You're on your honeymoon, which should be a work-free zone!

- Travel guides and maps of your destination.

- Your wedding ring. Do not—I repeat—do *not* forget to bring this important piece of jewelry with you on your honeymoon or you will face the wrath of your new bride!

Manage to forget something anyway? Don't stress. Most hotels offer essentials such as hair dryers, toothbrushes, toothpaste, combs, razors, shampoo, and conditioner. If not, you can likely pick up what you need at a nearby convenience store.

Now get out there, guys, and enjoy your honeymoon!

13

Writing Wedding Vows and Toasts

Nothing can strike fear into the hearts of men quite like having to give a speech—especially one to be delivered in front of a rather large group of people. Whether you're freaking out over—gulp—writing your own wedding vows or delivering your groom's speech on the big day, taking a little time to prepare yourself for your moment in the spotlight will help calm those nerves and eliminate any unhealthy fears.

Writing Your Own Vows

If traditional vows aren't your cup of tea and your officiant allows it, you and your fiancée may prefer to write your own vows for the wedding ceremony. This can be a great way to personalize your ceremony. Just keep in mind that it's also a very important undertaking that shouldn't be left to the last minute. You should begin working on them one to three months before the wedding.

Writing Tips

While writing vows comes naturally to some grooms, others may have a more difficult time putting their feelings into words. If you're not quite sure where to begin, start by jotting down some of the reasons why you love your fiancée, including a few of her best qualities and why you want to marry her. You might also include a favorite memory or anecdote, such as when you first met, your first date, or when you decided she was "the one."

There's nothing wrong with including some light humor, especially from a personal story (when appropriate)—but don't overdo it. Remember, you're writing vows to tell your fiancée how much you love her, rather than to entertain your guests. Heartfelt vows will come off as much classier to your fiancée and guests than humorous ones.

MAN DOWN
Writing your wedding vows isn't the time to be a comedian. Keep any jokes to a minimum, and whatever you do, make sure to keep them light and tasteful—unless you want to embarrass yourself and really tick off your bride-to-be. This is a wedding ceremony after all. Keep it classy, guys.

While complimenting her external beauty is a nice gesture, make sure to compliment her internal beauty and other personality traits as well so you don't come off sounding superficial. In addition, if there's a particular hymn, poem, or song you feel is appropriate, it might be nice to include a quote or verse from it.

Although the length of your vows is completely up to you, it's helpful to shoot for some sort of middle ground. While a couple of sentences will seem too short, don't include so much that you go overboard. This isn't a novel, after all. Stick to the main or most important points, and save the rest for love letters down the line.

Sample Self-Written Vows

Not quite sure where to start? Here are some sample wedding vows to help spark some ideas:

- [Bride's Name], as perfect as things are now, I know that life isn't always easy. I know that there will be ups and downs, triumphs and tragedies, successes and failures, wins and losses, good days and bad days. But I pledge to you that from this day forward, I'll always remain by your side, as your husband, your best friend, your confidante, your sounding board, and your biggest fan, cheering you on no matter what.

- [Bride's Name], when you suggested going to our alma mater's basketball game on our third date, I knew you were the perfect woman for me. Since then, we've grown up together and I can't wait to grow old with you.

- For the past five years, you've been there to support me and encourage my craziest ideas ... like entering that hot dog–eating contest (which I won, by the way) or going to the Amazon for an extreme fishing trip (I'm still working on that one). And today, I promise to always support you as my wife and best friend, even though your "crazy" ideas are much more practical and intelligent than mine.

- From the moment I met you, I knew I could always count on you and I want you to know that you can always count on me. I can't wait to become your husband and see where life will take us. I love you.

Practice, Practice, Practice

After you've devised your vows, practice saying them aloud in front of a mirror to perfect your timing and delivery. If something that seemed great on paper sounds strange when you say it out loud, revise it or consider scrapping it altogether. Also, make sure that you're comfortable saying everything you've included not only to your fiancée but also in front of your friends and family.

While nerves will likely come into play when you're reciting your vows at the ceremony, feeling prepared should help calm you down. If you plan to recite your vows from memory on the wedding day, practice saying them repeatedly both to yourself and aloud until you're able to recite them by heart.

 MAN DOWN
Although downing "liquid courage" may seem like a great way to ease your nerves before delivering your wedding vows, there's a difference between taking the edge off and overdoing it. Slurring or giggling your way through your vows will not only disappoint (as well as enrage) your fiancée but will also make you look like a total jerk in front of her family and friends. Don't be that guy. One drink or shot beforehand is fine, but any more is overkill.

However, if memorization seems a bit too risky, there's nothing wrong with having a few notes in tow. Jot down your vows word for word, or just write a few main bullet points on a note card to get you back on track in case you get wrapped up in the moment and lose your place. Prefer not to hang onto the note cards yourself? Have your best man keep a copy in his jacket pocket, and make sure he's prepared to slyly slip your cheat sheet to you during the ceremony in case you need it.

How to Handle Missteps

What if your mind goes blank at some point while you're delivering your vows? Take a deep breath and collect yourself. You'll likely remember your place (or can take a quick peek at your note card to jog your memory), but if not, just wing it. No one knows what you were going to say anyway, so don't worry if it doesn't come out exactly the way you planned it. Speak from your heart, and you'll do just fine.

If you still end up stumbling, making a mistake, laughing, or crying while delivering your vows, don't worry. This happens all the time at weddings—even to grooms. You're only human, and these moments will make the ceremony that much more endearing to your fiancée and guests.

Writing the Groom's Toast

As the groom, you'll most likely be expected at some point to deliver a toast that focuses on your bride as well as your families and guests. This toast is usually delivered at either the rehearsal dinner or wedding reception, depending on your preference, and is a great way to thank your family and friends for their support and/or involvement in your wedding.

An important speech that many people will remember, the groom's toast is typically delivered as the last toast of the evening. So whatever your plan, don't just wing it—make sure to take time to work on this speech beforehand.

When to Deliver

The timing and delivery of the groom's speech is up to each couple. If you're planning to open up time for speeches during the wedding reception, this is the perfect time for the groom's toast. However, if you and your fiancée prefer to have speeches at the rehearsal dinner instead (some couples do this to either keep things moving quickly and smoothly during the reception and/or to prevent any rowdy guests from embarrassing them in front of a larger group of people), the groom's speech can be delivered there as well.

If speeches are given at the rehearsal dinner, your parents (who are likely hosting this event) may start off the toasts, followed by your best man, maid-of-honor, and then you. If toasts are delivered at the wedding reception, the best man may begin the toasts, followed by the maid-of-honor, groom, and then family and friends. Sometimes the groom's toast can be the last speech of the evening at the reception as well. Keep in mind that there are no hard and fast rules on toast order. Discuss it with your fiancée beforehand, and feel free to incorporate your toast wherever you feel it's most appropriate.

MAN UP

Try your best to keep your groom's toast to two to five minutes. Remember, several other people will be or have already given toasts as well, and you don't want speeches to dominate the evening. The age-old advice applies here: keep your toast short and sweet, and give your guests some time to enjoy themselves.

Writing Tips

So what should you say in your toast? Here are a few ideas to get you started:

- Start by thanking everyone for coming. While many of your guests may live in town, others will be traveling long distances from other states or even other countries. Let them know that their presence is greatly appreciated and that you and your bride are thrilled that they could share in this special occasion with you.

- Thank both your family and your fiancée's family (or other appropriate family members) for their love, support, and involvement in your wedding plans. They played a major role in helping you become the people you are today, and chances are you couldn't have pulled off such an amazing wedding without them.

- Thank the members of your wedding party for their support and involvement in your big day as well. Not only have they likely attended countless wedding-related events, such as engagement parties, showers, and bachelor/bachelorette parties, and purchased attire and gifts for you, they've been there to support you along the way. Take the time to let them know you really appreciate them.

- Like in your wedding vows, make sure to keep humor at a minimum here. While a couple light jokes can work fine, it's best to leave the humorous toasts to your best man or maid-of-honor.

- Avoid mentioning controversial topics such as cultural issues, religion, or politics to prevent offending or embarrassing any guests. This isn't the time to spark a public debate.

- Your closing comments should focus on your bride. Take this time to let her know how much she means to you and how lucky you are to have her in your life.

Spend some time writing your speech at least a week or two before the wedding so you won't feel rushed slapping it together at the last minute. Then, practice your toast aloud several times before the big day so it sounds natural when you deliver it in person. Remember, you can always jot down a few points on a note card so you have something to fall back on if you happen to forget what you planned to say.

Sample Groom's Toast

If you're struggling with writer's block, take some inspiration from this groom's toast, delivered at the rehearsal dinner:

Good evening. [Bride's name] and I would like to thank all of you for coming tonight to celebrate with us. Some of you have come from around town, while others have come from across the globe, and we're so happy to be able to share this time in our lives with you.

Next, I'd like to thank both of our parents. They've always been there to love and support us and serve as great role models for us as we've grown up. They've been happily married for more than 45 years combined, and we hope to be just as fortunate. As you all can see, they've put a great deal of time and effort into planning the wedding celebrations for tonight and tomorrow, and we truly appreciate everything they've done for us. Cheers!

Next, I'd like to thank the bridesmaids for supporting [bride's name] and I and for their friendship over the years. They're a wonderful group of ladies I've had the pleasure to get to know over the last few years. I'd also like to thank the groomsmen, a group of guys with whom I play poker, watch sports, talk trash, and occasionally grab an O'Doul's. Right, Mom? They're a great group of guys that I've known for many years and I value their friendship. And for those of you who haven't met my brother and best man, [name], if there are any practical jokes played tomorrow, it's his fault and I should be informed about them immediately. On a serious note, you're my best friend and I appreciate your support. Cheers!

Finally, I want to thank [bride's name]. We met three years ago, became best friends, and fell in love. I'm so grateful to have you in my life every day. You're a funny, smart, and beautiful woman, who isn't too critical of my poor dancing skills, and I can't wait to marry you tomorrow. We've grown together over the last few years and I can't wait for what lies ahead in our future. I love you with all my heart. Cheers to you!

Can You Skip This Toast?

Although giving a groom's toast is a nice (and often expected) gesture, if you'd sooner jump out of a moving train than give a public speech, you could always skip it. Just don't be surprised if some guests give you a hard time about it later on.

But if at all possible, do your best to get over yourself, your nerves, and your stage fright and speak up. It will not only show your fiancée you're ready to man up but will also impress your family and friends.

Designating Others to Give Toasts

What about having other guests give toasts at your wedding? Make sure to either designate specific people to speak ahead of time or, if time isn't a major concern, open the floor to additional speeches after the wedding party and parents have spoken. Just make sure that someone, such as a DJ or band leader, cuts things off after a reasonable amount of time so that toasts don't end up dominating the evening.

Designating specific people to speak at your wedding, and having your DJ or band leader announce each of them before speaking, is also a good way to prevent random guests from jumping up and giving speeches, which could turn out to be embarrassing or inappropriate.

If you and your fiancée want a particular person—say, Uncle John—to give a speech at your wedding, make sure to let him know beforehand that you'd love for him to say a few words at your wedding reception or rehearsal dinner. Remember, no one likes to be put on the spot. Besides, the speeches will ultimately sound much better if your speakers are given time to prepare ahead of time.

MAN DOWN
If someone whom you or your fiancée would prefer *not* to speak at your wedding asks you beforehand whether he or she can give a speech, let the person down gently by blaming it on your tight timeline. Tell him or her that in order to keep things running smoothly during the evening, you've been forced to keep the wedding toasts to a minimum.

Also, take care when deciding who should deliver wedding toasts. For example, if you're very close with your cousin Joe but he always shares too much information or mentions old stories you wish he wouldn't, he probably isn't the best person to tap for a toast.

14

The Ceremony and Reception

Well, guys, it's official: you've made it to the wedding day, and the end game is now finally in sight. It's time to bid your single days farewell for good and become a happily married man. If you're like most guys, you're probably not quite sure what to expect on the day of the wedding. Don't worry. Here's a good overview of what your ceremony and reception will most likely entail so you won't feel clueless on the big day.

The Ceremony

By now, you've probably at least heard about the "I do" part when it comes to the wedding ceremony. But what the heck else is involved in the process? Whether you plan to have a religious or civil event, wedding ceremonies can vary depending on your personal preferences and any religious, cultural, or family traditions you want to incorporate.

What to Expect

When planning your wedding ceremony, make sure to discuss the typical timeline up front with your wedding officiant to make sure that everyone is on the same page in terms of expectations. If the bride wants both her father and step-father to walk her down the aisle, for example, inform your officiant about it. Prefer not to include the "'til death do us part" or "obey" line in your vows? Ask your officiant whether you can use another variation instead. Want to exit down the aisle to a rock song at the end of the ceremony? Find out whether it's acceptable. Considering using your dog as a ring bearer? See whether pets are allowed in the ceremony venue.

 MAN UP
Want to incorporate a few out-of-the-box elements in your wedding ceremony that are special to you and your bride? Check with your officiant and ceremony venue to see what's acceptable. While some marriage services may have little wiggle room, others may be more flexible. But of course, you'll never know unless you ask. Don't be afraid to speak up and see what's possible.

There may not be a great deal of leeway in some religious ceremonies, and almost all ceremony venues have their own set of rules and limitations—but it never hurts to see what else may be possible. If you're planning to have a less-traditional ceremony, you'll likely have much more flexibility to be as creative as you want with the itinerary. As always, just make sure to keep things classy ... it's a wedding, after all.

Typical Timeline

Although wedding ceremonies can vary depending on the type of service and other factors, here's a typical wedding ceremony timeline to give you a better idea of what yours may entail:

- **Giving in marriage.** After the bride has walked down the aisle, this is the part where the officiant usually says, "Who gives this woman in marriage?", and the father of the bride responds with either "I do" or "Her mother and I do."

- **Opening prayer, reading, or song.** Depending on the type of ceremony, this can be a prayer, scripture reading, poem, or song.

- **Definition of marriage.** The officiant will briefly talk about the meaning of marriage and why you've chosen to be married.

- **Vows.** (If you plan to craft your own vows, see Chapter 13 for writing tips.)

- **Second reading or song.**

- **Exchange of rings or gifts.**

- **Lighting of the unity candle** (optional, depending on ceremony type).

- **Closing.**

- **Declaration of marriage.**

- **Introduction of the newlyweds.**

Processional Order

You've already decided which family members and friends will make up your wedding party at this point, but when should each group of people walk down the aisle in your wedding ceremony? Your officiant will clue you in about the typical processional order for your type of service, and you'll also have a chance to walk your wedding party through the process during your rehearsal to clear up any last-minute confusion. But for a general idea of what to expect, here's a typical processional order for a church ceremony:

- Candle lighters (if applicable) enter and light candles for the ceremony.

- The bride and groom's grandparents and the groom's parents enter and are seated. (A related groomsman or usher typically escorts the grandmothers and mothers down the aisle.)

- The officiant and groom enter from the side (or through a side door) and wait at the altar.

- The groomsmen and bridesmaids walk down the aisle in pairs, beginning with those who will stand farthest away from the bride and groom and ending with the maid-/matron-of-honor and the best man (if applicable). In some ceremonies, the groomsmen also enter through a side door and only the bridesmaids walk down the aisle.

- The ring bearer and flower girl then proceed down the aisle.

- The bride and her father, both parents, or other designated person walk down the aisle.

- The bride typically stands on the left while the groom stands on the right.

Special Touches and Creative Ideas

Want to add a little something extra to your wedding ceremony? If your officiant and ceremony venue are open to it, there are many ways you can personalize your wedding ceremony, from the vows to the readings and music to finding unique ways to incorporate pets or children. Here are a few creative ideas to consider:

- Chat with your officiant about incorporating a special story about the two of you during the ceremony, such as how you met, what marriage means to you, or why you decided to get married.

- If allowed, consider reciting your own vows or incorporating special poems or songs that are meaningful to you and your bride.

- In place of a reading or right before it, have an important friend or family member say a few words about the two of you as a couple or why you're meant to be together.

- If you're musically inclined, consider writing and performing an original song during the ceremony.

- Light a special candle, hold a moment of silence, say a special prayer, or incorporate a flower arrangement in honor of a late family member or other important individual who is unable to attend (such as a sibling serving in the military or grandparent who is hospitalized). Or mention them in your wedding ceremony program.

- If acceptable, have a bridesmaid or groomsman walk Fido down the aisle as your ring bearer or honorary groomsman.

- Consider having the wedding party strike a pose just before they enter or even dance their way down the aisle.

- Release doves or butterflies at the end of the ceremony.

- Incorporate very young children into the ceremony by having an older flower girl or ring bearer slowly wheel them down the aisle in a wagon.

- Exit the ceremony venue in a classic vintage car (say, one owned by a family member) or a horse-drawn carriage to head to the reception in style.

Use your imagination to spark your own ideas that are meaningful to you and your bride. And, if you decide to stick with the more traditional route instead, go for it. There's definitely nothing wrong with that.

The Reception

Congrats, grooms! You've made it. Planning and organizing your wedding day may have been a wild ride, but now that the wedding ceremony is over, you're an officially married man—and it's time to enjoy your wedding reception.

What to Expect

Your reception is the time to kick back and celebrate your newlywed status with your wife (that's right—she's officially your wife now!), family, and friends—in the form of a kick-ass party, of course. Depending on the type of reception you've chosen to organize, you and your guests should expect to enjoy some form of the following: cocktails and hors d'oeuvres; a full buffet or plated meal; open bars, cash bars, or other refreshments; music and dancing; mingling; cake-cutting; speeches or toasts; and general celebrating.

While your wedding reception vendors will no doubt be at your disposal in arranging all the various details of this celebration, you and your fiancée will likely be in charge of determining the order of events for the evening and adding any personal elements you would like to make your reception extra meaningful and memorable for both you and your guests.

Typical Timeline

Of course, just as no two wedding ceremonies are exactly alike, wedding receptions are often unique to the couples who plan them. The reception timeline is up to you to coordinate with your vendors and can most likely be arranged in virtually any way you see fit.

However, if you're not sure what to include or in what order, here's a quick breakdown of common reception elements:

- Announcement of the newlyweds. Typically, your band or DJ will announce you and your new bride to your guests as you first enter the reception venue.

- Time for the cocktail hour, meal, or other refreshments

- Speeches or toasts

- Cake-cutting

- Champagne toast (optional)

- Dancing

- Greeting and mingling with guests

- Handing out send-off materials

- Grand exit

Party Hard (But Don't Go Overboard)

Your wedding reception is definitely a great time to hang loose, relax, and celebrate. For many guys, it's also time to get your drink on. If you plan to celebrate with alcohol, by all means have a few drinks. Just don't go overboard. If you don't know how to have a good time without overdoing it by now, it's time to man up and grow up. That said, if you have to enlist your best man to cut you off after a certain number of drinks, do it.

We've all heard horror stories of grooms who overindulged and later either slurred their way through their toast (much to the chagrin of their new bride); shared too many sensitive, personal details with guests (such as, "Sarah's preggers, so her folks said we had to get hitched!"); managed to fall off the dance floor; took an accidental plunge in the pool outside the reception venue; or simply ended up acting like a complete jackass. Please don't let this be you. Enjoy yourself responsibly, and keep things classy.

MAN DOWN
Don't forget to take the time to eat at your wedding reception. Believe it or not, many newlywed couples quickly get swept away mingling with guests right after they arrive at their receptions and never have a chance to sit down and eat. After such a long day, you'll both need sustenance, and you should take some time to eat, drink, and enjoy everything you've arranged. Keep in mind that you're on a schedule, though, and shouldn't linger at your table longer than necessary. Carve out time to celebrate the day together over a quick bite before moving on with the festivities.

Eat, Drink, and Be Merry

While you and your new bride can eat at any point during the reception, your guests will expect to be able to eat and drink right away. If you're not planning to offer a cocktail hour with hors d'oeuvres before the main meal (or before you arrive, if you'll be entering a bit later after taking photos with the wedding party), make sure to open the buffet or have staff take meal orders soon after the reception begins so that guests don't get hungry while they're waiting.

A word of caution: although some couples prefer to greet guests and mingle before eating, this often results in them not having a chance to eat at all during their wedding reception. I highly recommend sitting down for a bite to eat right after you've arrived so you both have a chance to enjoy the fruits of your labor. Then, proceed with the next step in your reception plans.

Cutting the Cake and the Champagne Toast

Whether you're planning to have a traditional wedding cake, groom's cake, cupcakes, doughnuts, or other sweet treats at your wedding reception, you and your wife will be expected to cut and share a piece together as a newly married couple. According to traditional etiquette, the bride and groom typically feed each other a piece of cake (arm-crossing and all, if you like)—but like many other wedding traditions, this one's up to you. Also make sure your new wife is into smashing cake in each other's faces if that's the route you plan to go, but I'd suggest the much more civil (and classier) approach of feeding each other a piece instead. Your wait staff will then serve cake (or other desserts) to your guests or set plates out for guests to take if they choose.

Although optional, if you're planning to include a champagne toast at your reception, it can be a great complement to the cutting of the cake—especially if you're not planning to have any other toasts or speeches during your reception. Once champagne is served to you and your guests, your DJ or band leader (or other designated person) will ask everyone to raise their glasses and toast the newlyweds. Again, you and your bride can choose whether or not you want to cross arms while you enjoy your first sip of champagne. And if you and your new wife don't drink, just raise a glass of your non-alcoholic drink of choice instead. After all, the toast is the main point, not the drink.

 CHA-CHING
Looking for an easy way to save on alcohol costs at your wedding reception? Skip the champagne toast. Although it may be a nice gesture, serving champagne to each of your guests can also be quite costly. Let guests toast with whatever drink they already have in hand instead. Champagne is a non-essential item you can easily cut to save some dough without guests noticing.

Speeches or Toasts

If delivered at the wedding reception (instead of at the rehearsal dinner, for example), toasts are typically given during meal service once guests have been seated. If you plan to designate speakers ahead of time, your DJ or band leader will announce each person and their relationship to you before they deliver their toast. Otherwise, once your DJ or band opens the floor to speeches, he or she may need to cut things off at a certain point if the toasts start running too long.

My recommendation: designate people to give toasts ahead of time to keep speeches to a minimum and ensure that the reception runs on time. (For more details on speeches and toasts, see Chapter 13.)

Dancing

If you and your bride plan to cut a rug with your guests at your wedding reception, your band or DJ will likely open the dance floor with your first dance, followed by any other designated dances you choose, and then extend the invitation to the rest of your guests to join.

Not sure which dances to include? Here are the most common wedding-reception dances to consider:

- **First dance.** This is the bride and groom's first dance together as a married couple. This is typically the first dance of the evening, before the DJ opens the floor for guests to join.

- **Mother-son dance.** If applicable, the mother-son and father-daughter dances are great ones to include to share some one-on-one time with the family members who raised you and to thank them for their contribution to your wedding.

- **Dollar dance, chicken dance, wedding-party dance, or anniversary dance (optional).** Many couples either love or hate these types of dances, so once again, the choice is up to you. Although some people may think it's tacky, if you'd love to get some extra cash for the honeymoon, you might want to consider incorporating a dollar dance, where guests pay a dollar (or whatever additional amount they choose) to dance with the bride and groom for a minute. Does your wedding party love group dances? This could be a great way to cater to that with a special wedding-party dance. For the anniversary dance, your band or DJ will invite married guests to dance and later announce that only those married for 5 years, 10 years, 20 years, and so on, can stay on the floor. This can be a nice way to highlight the marriages of your parents, grandparents, and other guests.

Dance Moves to Impress

If you don't already have mad dance skills, don't sweat it. You and your bride can take a dance lesson or two before the wedding to brush up on your moves and eliminate your two left feet. Or, if you don't have a problem getting your groove on in a club but can't stomach the thought of dancing in front of all your friends and family, dance lessons can also help you become more confident and ease your nerves. This can also be a great way for you and your bride to spend some time together and unwind a bit before the big day arrives.

Whether you decide to go with a more traditional dance or spice things up with some salsa moves, don't be afraid to go for it. Along with the song you choose for your first dance (see Appendix B for some great song choices to consider), this is another area where you can personalize your wedding and make it memorable for guests.

Garter Removal Tips

You know the drill by now. Your bride typically sits on a chair, and you kneel down to carefully remove the garter from her leg. Of course, music will be played throughout the process, so discuss song options beforehand with your band or DJ to select the type of song you prefer.

Want to spice things up a bit? First, talk to your bride to make sure she's game with going outside the norm here. (Ending up in the doghouse during the reception can result in a less-than-stellar wedding night, which is definitely something you want to avoid at all costs.) Use your imagination. Want to dance on your way over to your bride? Go for it. Considering donning a head lamp? Well, it *is* dark underneath that wedding dress. Whatever you decide, have a good time and your guests will get a kick out of it as well.

Incorporating Traditions

Religious, cultural, and other family traditions can be incorporated at any point during the wedding reception as you see appropriate. For example, at a Jewish wedding reception, newlywed couples typically incorporate a Hora or chair dance, where guests lift up the bride and groom on chairs above the crowd while singing and dancing. At a Christian wedding, a minister or priest may give a blessing at the beginning of the reception, before the meal is served.

Traditions are a great way to personalize your reception and make it even more unique and memorable for both your family and guests. Feel free to incorporate any traditions that are meaningful to you and your bride.

Taking Time to Chat with Guests

Although it may sound obvious, make sure that you and your wife take time to visit with as many guests as possible at some point during your wedding reception. What you've heard is true—your reception will go by very quickly, and it's easy to get caught up running around from place to place while you're dancing, cutting the cake, and so on. But don't overlook this important step.

Likewise, don't spend the entire reception chatting with your wedding party, closest friends, or only those at your table. Make an effort to greet or talk to someone at each table so that everyone feels like an important guest. While speaking with every single guest may not be possible if you plan to have a large reception, do your best to make everyone feel welcome and let them know that you appreciate their presence.

Special Touches and Creative Ideas

Looking for some unique ways to personalize your wedding reception and really wow your guests? Take inspiration from some of these creative ideas:

- Use a projector and screen to display a video or photo slideshow (with the volume turned off) that includes images of you and your bride growing up as children and then of you as a couple. This is also a great place to incorporate your engagement photos.

- Designate an area on the reception floor to display family wedding photos from both sets of parents and grandparents. Both families will really appreciate this sentimental gesture. This can also be a nice way to incorporate photos of loved ones who have passed away.

- Want to include your pet, but he or she can't physically be present at the reception? Set out a photo of your pet in a designated area (such as near the gift table) to let guests know this important guest isn't forgotten.

- Highlight your love of your favorite sports team, hobby, profession, or hometown with a themed groom's cake. This is a great personal touch that can inject some masculinity and whimsicality into your reception. (For more details on groom's cakes and cake design ideas, see Chapter 8.)

- Want to go beyond placing disposable cameras at each table for guests to use? Consider renting a photo or video booth so guests can capture fun moments throughout the night. Bonus: you'll have the video footage afterward so you can relive the reception memories for years to come.

- Create a candy bar for guests to enjoy. Fill different-size glass canisters with your favorite candies or other treats. Also, set out scoops and monogrammed bags so guests can take some sweets home at the end of the evening.

Of course, feel free to come up with your own unique ideas to really make your reception stand out from the norm.

A Man Cave at Your Wedding Reception?

What if there's a major sporting event going on during your wedding reception? Of course, the wedding must go on. But don't hesitate to carve out a small area of the reception venue (or just outside it) to create a "man cave" that male guests can visit periodically to check in on the score or just chill out and relax for a bit.

Equip your man-cave area with comfy seating, a large-screen TV, and of course a bar nearby. This area can be tented off so it doesn't interfere with the rest of the reception, but it will be a welcome respite to your die-hard sports-fan guests. Of course, don't be surprised if a few women drop in as well.

How to Spot and Bust a Wedding Crasher

If you're like most guys, you've probably seen the movie *Wedding Crashers* by now. (If not, I highly recommend watching it as a pre-wedding stress reliever.) Although the movie is hilarious, now that you're the one getting married you might be wondering how you'd handle things if an uninvited guest managed to get into your wedding.

So what's a dude to do in this situation? Of course, as the size of your guest list swells, the chances of spotting a wedding crasher may become more difficult. One way to prevent crashers is to enlist a friend or relative to keep an eye on guests as they enter the ceremony venue (such as the guest book or program attendant), as well as someone (such as the gift table attendant) to look out for uninvited guests as they enter the reception. Another option is to have a security guard check guests who enter against a guest list; although this may seem a bit extreme, it may come in especially handy for warding off uninvited ex-spouses/girlfriends or estranged parents who could upset your bride or other guests by showing up unannounced.

However, if crashers do find their way into your wedding, you can either designate a guest (I'd suggest using someone who's football player–sized) or security guard to escort them out—or, as a last resort, call the police. My recommendation: have someone at your wedding handle it rather than calling the police to prevent startling your other (invited) guests and ruining the atmosphere of an otherwise great party.

Grand Exit

At long last, this is the home stretch, guys! Once your reception has come to an end, you and your wife will make your exit and head to your wedding-night destination to celebrate your first night together as a married couple.

If you plan to give guests send-off materials or favors that aren't already placed at their tables or near the door as they exit, you may want to have your band or DJ announce special instructions to guests, such as taking sparklers, bottles of bubbles, or flower petals from a communal area with them to shower you upon your exit.

The Wedding Night

Well, there you are. The wedding reception is over and you're alone with your bride—finally. The wedding day will really take a toll on you and your bride. You're bound to be dead tired after hours of standing, posing, dancing, and talking to every family member and friend at the reception. Chances are you'll also be a little tipsy due to the empty-hand policy. (If you're not familiar with this dangerously glorious policy, it's the understood rule among guys that anyone catching the groom with an empty hand at the reception must get him a drink.) Score!

Given the exhaustion factor, no one could blame you if you decided to head home or go straight to the hotel to pass out. However, if you're up to it, there's still some fun to be had post-wedding. Whether you're continuing the party with your friends or getting a head start on the honeymoon with your bride, there is definitely a strategy for making the most of your wedding night.

After the Reception

As mentioned in the previous chapter, you and your bride probably have a grand reception exit planned. I encourage you to make this as legendary as possible but also not to forget to say goodbye to both sets of parents and other family members. Doing this might be as simple as pulling them aside before you walk out the door. However, for you sentimentalists out there, an alternative idea is a short meet-up afterward in a spare hotel room or nearby coffee shop. If you're leaving for the honeymoon early the next morning, this option will suit you well because there won't be time for breakfast or brunch beforehand. This meet-up will give you and your bride the opportunity to be a little more personal with your goodbyes and thank-yous. And while this may seem like a buzz kill, it will most certainly be appreciated.

MAN DOWN

Although your friends will attempt to hand you a drink each time they catch you with an empty hand at the reception, it's important to pace yourself. And yes, it's okay to say no. The last thing you want is to not be able to walk out of the wedding reception and enjoy the wedding night on your own two feet.

After the reception, it's up to you and your bride to decide where the night goes next. While traditionally thought of as a night for lovers only, it has quietly become the norm for couples to opt to continue drinking and dancing with friends well into the night and early hours of the next morning. You've probably been to a wedding where the groom and bride led a march to a favorite bar or club after their exit from the reception. And it probably was a lot of fun due to the fact that it gave you the opportunity to visit and share a drink with the newlyweds—something you probably didn't have a chance to do at the wedding (because they were kind of busy).

If a wedding night on the town fits your style as a couple, I say go for it. There's no golden rule that says you have to be alone with your new bride all night. You've got the rest of your life to spend with your lady. If you're the type of couple that puts an added emphasis on spending time with friends and enjoying a good party, make the most of it. It is *your* wedding night, after all.

Here are my top five suggestions for post-reception partying:

- Lead a caravan to you and your bride's favorite go-to night spot. Take advantage of one of the few nights in your life when everything is on the house.

- A group bowling, miniature golf, or casino outing will keep the fun going well into the night. This is a nice option if some members of your group aren't into the bar scene.

- Want to feel like a rock star? How about hitting up a favorite local karaoke club? Trust me, you and your new wife will never feel as popular again as you will when you're belting out "Don't Stop Believin'" in your wedding day get-up.

- See whether your hotel or reception site has a private room you can rent for a few hours. Keeping everything at a central location will help your after-party run more smoothly.

- Host a small after-party at your place. This gives you the opportunity to change and get cleaned up after a night of sweating, although I guarantee your bride will stay in her dress all night!

On the flip side, if you have an early honeymoon flight or family obligation the next day, there's no reason your friends can't keep the party alive on their own. Be sure to let your guests know where the hot spots in town are (preferably closer to the reception site or hotels). In addition to bar information, you should also provide phone numbers to local cab companies. We've all been to weddings and know how quickly booze can flow. There's no reason to take a risk on what should be a night of cheerful celebration. A good place to share all this information is on your wedding website or inside your guest welcome bags.

MAN UP
Taking off on the honeymoon the day after the wedding and still want to hit the town with your friends for the after-party? Try to book the latest flight possible, or consider leaving yourself a few days between the wedding and the honeymoon. You don't want to start off the honeymoon completely and utterly exhausted.

Wedding Night Pranks

Another thing to be on the lookout for during the wedding day, and more specifically that night, is pranks. Of course, it goes without saying that one of the best man's unwritten duties is to have a little fun with the groom through some sort of prank. These pranks are all in good fun, of course, until the bride gets involved. What you may see as "clowning around" by your buddies, she might see as a blemish on her perfect wedding day. This is why it's important to not tell anyone where you're staying on the wedding night. Let me repeat that. Do *not* tell anyone where you are staying on the wedding night! This is a precaution that simply has to be taken to prevent a rogue groomsman from planning something sinister involving the honeymoon suite, room phone, or worse … a video camera. By the way, if you were wondering where to stay on the wedding night, check out the handy chart on the following page to see what most couples do.

It would be wise to let your buddies know that while you certainly appreciate a little ribbing earlier in the day, the wedding night should be off limits. If you're afraid of sounding like a sissy, don't be. Just do what I did and blame it on the bride! And be sure to let them know that any late-night debauchery will be returned two-fold.

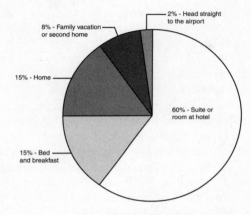

2% - Head straight to the airport

8% - Family vacation or second home

15% - Home

60% - Suite or room at hotel

15% - Bed and breakfast

Where do newlyweds stay on the wedding night?

Sex: Does It Actually Happen?

Wondering whether you and your new bride will be too wiped out to score on your wedding night? If you're like 45 percent of newlyweds, the answer to this question is yes. With the wedding-day schedule being ridiculously busy and exhausting, no one could blame you if you decide to go back home or to the hotel to simply crash. However, if you're one of the lucky 55 percent: game on! Planning the perfect wedding-night romp starts by making sure you're rested up and have plenty of energy.

If you're forgoing a post-party with friends, it's wise to chill out and relax for a bit after the wedding. But be careful, there's a fine line between resting to recoup energy and falling asleep. Chances are you'll spend the first hour or so after the reception reminiscing about the wedding day and how great it was. I also recommend having a doggy bag prepared for both of you with food from the reception. This is a standard practice with most caterers. Because most couples are too busy to eat very much during the day, food will replenish your body for the more strenuous activities to come. Check with your wedding planner or put someone in charge of making sure the doggy bags end up in your hands as you're leaving the reception. In addition to eating, it's also important to hydrate yourself as much as possible.

TRADITION SAYS

You're surely familiar with the image of the groom carrying the bride over the threshold and into their home for the first time as husband and wife. But do you know the reason why that's straight out of "Dungeons & Dragons"? According to ancient beliefs, by carrying her over the threshold, you'll ward off any demons that she's bringing into the marriage from her side of the family. As for your demons … well, you're on your own, pal.

Virgins? Don't Stress!

If you'll be a virgin up until your wedding night, I have two things to say: first, congrats on your accomplishment, and second, don't forget that it can help to do a little research ahead of time. There are definitely some tips to make that first time a little less "anxiety- and fear-filled" and a little more "shock and awe." People remain virgins until marriage for many reasons, and for whatever yours may be, you should be commended. It isn't an easy choice—but one that will reward you in the future. Remember, all good things come to those who wait.

At this point, you should already be comfortable talking about sex with your fiancée. If not, now's the time to bring it up. This is a very simple way to cut through any tension and or anxiety. If she's a virgin as well, you'll both be experiencing this together and can discuss your feelings and expectations. Most couples will also attend some sort of pre-marriage counseling, and this is another place that sex will probably be discussed—so it helps to be prepared ahead of time.

While women can definitely enjoy their first time, it's important to remember that this isn't one of those dirty movies that you hid under your bed when you were a teenager. She probably won't appreciate any crazy, kung fu–type moves on your wedding night. It's always a good idea to lube it up and take your time with some pre-dance moves (otherwise known as foreplay), such as massaging and kissing.

Losing your virginity to your bride is a great thing. Just remember to communicate with her long before the big night. This will help dissolve any anxiety you may have. Also, remember to continue the communication into the bedroom so you'll both learn what you like and how you can help her have a great time.

 MAN UP
Things can get a little tricky if she's a virgin and you're not. If this describes your situation, it's wise to be honest with her about your sexual past and number of partners. There should be no secrets in marriage, especially in the bedroom. Be the man, and be honest!

Sex Tips and Setting the Mood

For some guys, all the pressure of bringing your A-game mixed with all the stress of the wedding day might have you a little worried. Remember, proper planning prevents poor performance. Here are some tips for making the most of your wedding night:

- Since you'll (hopefully) never get another shot at wedding-night sex, make it an experience that will be hard to top. Whether you're staying at a hotel or at home, plan ahead and have some rose petals, chocolate-covered strawberries, champagne, or a combination of the three prepared in the bedroom. I don't expect you to fully understand, but women dig this kind of stuff (especially brides).

Another way to set the mood is to create an iPod mix or CD of songs that have meant a lot to you and your bride over the years. Of course, make sure to pick songs that won't get old—because you'll hopefully be hearing them on repeat all night long!

- Talk dirty to her. Of course, I'm talking about telling your brand-new wife how special she is and how beautiful she looked in her wedding dress. Nothing will likely get your bride in the mood more than hearing this. She has been looking forward to this day for quite some time. From there, the conversation can turn to more arousing material.

- Be a gentleman and gently help her out of her wedding dress. Hey, if you're lucky, she may just end up helping you out of your tux (and whatever lies beneath).

- Who said that sex has to wait until after the reception? If you have a spare moment or two between the ceremony or reception, maybe you can duck away for a few minutes to get the party started early. Just be sure to be quick. The last thing you want is for someone to file a missing-persons report for you on your wedding day.

- If you and your fiancée are already having sex, consider taking a break until the wedding night. This won't be easy, but it will be rewarding. The longer the break you can survive, the more satisfying the wedding night will be. I've heard of some couples going as long as a year between having sex last and the wedding night. That's almost like becoming a virgin again! Maybe a more realistic goal is two months sans sex. It won't be easy, so give yourselves a mulligan or two. Accidents do happen.

- For those men out there who like to boldly go where few others have gone before, try wearing something special for her. That's right, sexy attire isn't limited to the "hers" section. Whether it's a pair of leopard-print boxers or maybe a themed costume that will fulfill a fantasy that she's always dreamed of, the key here is to be creative.

MAN DOWN
Whatever you plan for the wedding night, don't forget the champagne. Champagne has been proven to be a natural aphrodisiac, so you would be doing yourself quite the disservice by leaving it off your honeymoon suite menu. Bottoms up!

- Study up on sex moves and positions that you'd like to try. You don't have to become an expert on the *Kama Sutra*, but trying something new and exciting might add to the experience of the wedding night.

- Don't forget to stop for a moment to take it all in. In 50 years, you'll look back on the wedding night and wish you could relive it. Live in the moment, and enjoy the night to its fullest potential.

You know your bride-to-be better than me. Use this information as a jumping-off point for planning your big night. The main thing to remember is to make your bride feel special. If you can do that, you'll succeed. As far as your performance, don't put any unnecessary expectations on yourself. Most likely, you won't be Superman but more like Clark Kent. The idea is to enjoy the night with your bride. Take things slowly unless you're so tired that you're ready to fall asleep. If that's the case, don't sweat it. Remember, 45 percent of couples don't close the deal on their wedding night, so if you're both exhausted, don't feel like you have to. Trust me, there will be plenty of time for that during the honeymoon.

Lingerie

By the time the wedding night rolls around, you'll probably have given your new bride some form of a wedding-day gift. Whether it's jewelry, a framed photo, or some other sentimental gift, she'll surely love it. However, you might be able to one-up yourself by having a new pair of underwear or piece of lingerie awaiting her for the wedding night or honeymoon. If she's comfortable in negligee, treat her (and yourself) right.

If you're like most guys (myself included), you don't particularly care for venturing into the women's underwear shop alone. Never fear—you can always purchase lingerie from the comfort of your own home via the Internet. If you're a lingerie novice, this might prove tricky without actually being able to ask any questions. To help get you started, here's a quick breakdown of some popular types of lingerie:

- If you're unfamiliar with thongs and G-strings, I've got to ask whether you're ready to be getting married. Nonetheless, the thong became famous for being underwear that leaves her behind exposed (and supposedly to eliminate panty lines, so I've heard). The G-string takes it to the next level by only covering her backside with a thin strip of material. Pretty cool, right?

- You probably have experience with the baby doll because it's one of the most common pieces of lingerie. It most commonly resembles a short-cut dress and is generally made of silk, nylon, or other sheer material.

- A teddy is known for resembling a one-piece bathing suit. But trust me, fellas, this has nothing to do with swimming. They're commonly made of lace and combine a camisole and underwear into one sexy piece of lingerie.

- The corset is probably the most formal piece of lingerie. It's also the oldest, dating back to the 1500s. You'll know it best by the amazing cleavage that it displays. Today's corsets are a little more comfortable for her than those worn by queens of medieval times. They can also include garter straps that add to the sexiness of the attire.

$ CHA-CHING

Does your family own a lake house, cabin, or other nearby vacation home? Consider spending the wedding night at one of these locations, as opposed to shelling out beaucoup bucks for an expensive hotel suite that you'll only be in for a few hours.

One Groom's Story
Derek in Albuquerque

Derek and his bride, Sara, wanted a big wedding. They both came from big families and knew that their guest list would be well in excess of 250 family members and friends. They also knew it would be a near impossibility to personally visit with everyone in attendance beyond the obligatory quick "thank you for coming" hug or handshake. This posed a problem, as they boasted a close-knit circle of friends—some of whom would be coming from across the country to be there for the wedding. It simply wasn't acceptable to Derek and Sara to not get in quality celebrating time with their crew. Instead of stressing out about it, they devised a plan to put together an after-party that would give them an opportunity to visit with their friends and still have time to do the traditional wedding-night "stuff."

In the weeks before the wedding, Derek instructed his best man to start spreading the word to the wedding party and other friends about a wedding post-party at a local bar. Sara enlisted her maid-of-honor to do the same. The couple also reserved a private room at the bar that could accommodate the group. The kicker is that outside of the best man and maid-of-honor, no one would know that the newlyweds would be dropping in on the party. To their friends, the post-party was just an extension of the celebration after they closed down the reception bar.

I'm sure you can imagine the rock-star feeling that Derek and Sara had as they walked into the party and surprised all of their friends. They drank and mingled for several hours and then made their exit and headed back to an undisclosed location to enjoy the rest of the wedding night—alone.

Legal Issues

Bravo for getting to this point, guys. I'm guessing you probably didn't immediately skip to this chapter like you may have done with the bachelor party chapter. (And I can't say that I blame you there.) But trust me—this chapter is no less important in terms of preparing yourself for your wedding and married life.

Legal issues don't exactly make for sexy reading material, but simply ignoring them could land you in an incredibly tight spot as well as potentially derail your wedding plans (and no one wants that). So please, stay with me here. You might just learn something that could save you a major headache later.

Marriage Licenses

To legally get hitched, you'll first need to apply for and obtain a marriage license. This is something the groom typically obtains and purchases. Your first step should be to check with your county or state regarding its marriage license requirements.

Some states have different requirements than others, so if you're getting married just over the state line, don't assume that the rules will be the same. For example, while some states require both the groom and bride to be present to obtain the marriage license, other states require only one party to be present. In some states, you may even be able to apply for a license by mail. Certain states may also require a blood test to be administered before you can apply for a marriage license.

 TRADITION SAYS

According to etiquette, the groom typically handles acquiring and purchasing the marriage license before the wedding. Getting married in another state? Make sure you arrive early enough to apply for and obtain your license. Many states impose a one- to seven-day waiting period between the time you can apply for and retrieve your license.

To give you an idea of what to expect, some typical marriage license requirements may include the following:

- **Identification.** Some states require some combination of the following: applicants' driver's licenses, passports, visas, military ID or other state-issued ID, Social Security numbers, certified birth certificates, both applicants' fathers' and mothers' full names and places of birth, and the name and address of the officiant performing the ceremony.

- **Residency.** Some states may require you to be a resident of the state in order to obtain a marriage license (while others don't).

- **Previous marriages.** If you or your bride were previously divorced or widowed, you'll need to provide the county, state, and date and may also need to provide a divorce decree or death certificate.

- **Application.** In some states, the applicant(s) (bride, groom, or both) must appear in person and swear under oath that the applicants aren't related, have no spouse, and are aware of no other reason why they shouldn't be legally married. Other states may allow applicants to apply via mail using signed, notarized affidavits.

- **Waiting period.** Some states require a one- to seven-day waiting period between the time you apply for your license and can pick it up.

- **Blood tests.** Some states also require blood tests or physical exams.

- **Age.** In some states, if either applicant is younger than age 18, he or she must provide a certified birth certificate—and either both living parents or legal guardians must be present or the applicant may be able to produce notarized, written consent from all living parents or guardians. Or, he or she may provide notarized, written consent from one parent or guardian and consent of a district court judge.

- **Witnesses.** Some states require that one or two people (typically the maid-of-honor and best man) witness the marriage ceremony and sign the marriage license after the ceremony is performed.

- **Name change.** Some states require the bride to list her choice of last name on the marriage certificate.

- **Fees.** Applicants are typically charged a fee between $5 and $100 to obtain a marriage license. Often, only cash is accepted. However, some states will waive or discount application fees if the applicants have completed several hours of premarital education classes.

When and Where to Get It

Although each state is different, you can expect to obtain your marriage license somewhere between a week up to a few months prior to your wedding. Make sure to find out how long your license will be valid before you apply for it. Marriage licenses are typically valid for 30 days up to a year, depending on the state. (Most clergy members or court officials will not marry you without a valid marriage license.)

MAN DOWN
Believe it or not, it's possible to obtain your marriage license too early. Although some marriage licenses are valid for 6 to 12 months, many others are only valid for 30 days. Make sure to be aware of your license's expiration date. This is one major wedding foul you don't want to commit.

In most states, you can apply for and acquire your marriage license at the county or city courthouse or clerk's office.

An ordained clergy member, current or retired district court judge, justice of a court of record, or municipal judge can legally perform wedding ceremonies. The officiant must sign the marriage certificate after the ceremony is performed and send it in to the county or state agency to be recorded.

Obtaining a Certified Copy of Your Marriage Certificate

In some states, married couples may be provided with one free certified copy of their marriage certificate after the officiant has turned it in to the state. However, in other states, couples must contact the county courthouse to request and pay for certified copies.

You'll need to acquire this document to legally change your bride's name after the wedding (more on that later in this chapter). I recommend obtaining two copies of your marriage certificate, just in case one happens to get damaged or misplaced. It's also a good idea to keep one copy in a safety-deposit box so you'll always know where it is.

Destination Weddings: Know Your Country's Policies

If you're planning a destination wedding, you'll need to research your country's marriage license requirements ahead of time. Although you'll likely need to bring similar identification documents as you would in the United States, foreign countries often impose different requirements for couples to legally marry.

Here are a few common foreign marriage requirements to be aware of:

- The legal age of consent may be older than 18 in certain countries.

- Some countries may require you and your bride to arrive or "reside" in the country for a few (usually one to five) days prior to your wedding ceremony before you can legally be married.

- In certain countries, you must mail in necessary forms (such as a "Notice of Intent to Marry") a couple weeks before your wedding takes place.

- Some countries may require that you have at least four witnesses present to validate your wedding ceremony.

- Other countries may require that you be married in a specific type of religious ceremony, so make sure that's acceptable to you.

- Certain countries may request that your identification documents be translated into the local language and notarized.

- Some countries require you to present a return ticket home, so it's important to book round-trip tickets ahead of time.

- License application fees may also cost more in foreign countries.

Of course, you and your bride (as well as your guests) will likely need a valid passport and perhaps also a visa to enter certain countries, so make sure to determine your destination's policies for entry beforehand and also inform your guests accordingly.

Prenups

Wondering whether you and your bride should sign a prenuptial agreement before you get married? Nothing can stir up a debate quicker among engaged couples than the notorious prenup conversation. However, having this discussion doesn't mean that you're expecting to get a divorce down the line. In fact, it can be a smart move for both you and your soon-to-be wife to discuss what would happen to your assets if something happened to one of you or if you ended up getting a divorce.

Let's face it: many couples today are getting married later in life and are typically in a better financial situation now than they were during their 20s. And, of course, most guys have heard about the dreaded 50 percent divorce rate. Additionally, some grooms (or brides) may stand to inherit money from late family members, own real estate, or own a business with their parents or siblings and need to protect their assets in case the marriage doesn't work out. Whatever your reasons, prenups may make sense for some couples.

Broaching the Subject

Although bringing up the prenup with your bride can be a sticky situation, the sooner you broach the subject, the better. If you wait until the last minute to discuss it, you might run out of time to have the agreement drawn up and signed before the wedding day.

If it's something that's important to you, you'll need to talk it over with your bride. However, keep in mind that she may not be incredibly open to the idea. While no one wants to admit that their marriage may not last forever, divorce may not be the only reason to get a prenup. What if you were to die in a car accident, for example? It's important to have a plan in place for the distribution of your assets. Make sure she knows that getting a prenup doesn't have to mean that one person is "worth more" than the other or that you're afraid of "getting screwed in a divorce" later on. It's simply a way for both of you to protect yourselves in the event that the unthinkable happens.

This can also be a good time to discuss both your and your bride's financial situations before you tie the knot. Many couples wait until after they're married to discuss how they'll handle their finances. Is one of you bringing lots of debt or student loans into the marriage? Talking about this during the prenup process will help open that dialog much sooner so you can address any issues before they get worse.

Talking to a Lawyer

Whether getting a prenup is something your family is pressuring you to do or something you want to do on your own to protect yourself, you should plan to speak with an attorney to learn more about your options. A lawyer can walk you through the different types of prenup agreements that can be created and the advantages and disadvantages of each.

You and your bride may want to obtain separate legal counsel to make sure that both of your desires are taken into account during the process. Once you're finished, you'll both have peace of mind and can move on with the rest of your wedding plans.

Tax Implications

Concerned about the marriage tax penalty once April rolls around? While this tax penalty still exists to some extent, it's not necessarily as bad as you may have heard.

The reality is that combining both of your incomes may push you into a higher tax bracket as a married couple. However, if one of you earns significantly less than the other, you may actually save money by filing together because some of the higher earner's income will be pulled into a lower tax bracket.

Once you're legally married, you'll have the option of submitting your taxes as "married filing jointly" or "married filing separately." Although it may sound counter-intuitive, you may not actually save money by going the "married filing separately" route.

MAN UP
If your bride decided to change her name after you got married, make sure she updates her name with the Social Security Administration (SSA) before filing your taxes so it matches your return. Otherwise, they'll delay your refund check until the name discrepancy is sorted out.

If you work with an accountant or tax service, I'd recommend discussing your tax options with them to see what makes the most sense for you and your wife. And, if you file your taxes on your own, make sure to research which option best fits your current situation.

Changing the Bride's Name

To some couples, changing the bride's last name is a no-brainer. To others, it can be a slightly more difficult proposition. Some more-traditional guys may feel that if his bride doesn't take his last name, it's a deal-breaker. Other guys don't care a bit. They may feel that as long as you're married, that's all that really matters.

Talking Her Into It

If she's not crazy about it and it's important to you, keep in mind that being forced to change her last name may not only seem strange and unnecessary (she has had the same last name for her entire life until now) but also a bit sexist to her. "Why don't you have to change *your* name?" she might wonder.

One reason for her to take your name is to keep things simpler if you have children. For example, it could be confusing later on when Mr. Johnson comes to pick up Ms. Carter's children from school. Strangers may also incorrectly assume that you're just dating if you both have different last names. It can also make things easier for both of you when you need to get important information from your insurance company, doctor's office, bank, and so on, if you both have the same last name.

If she still isn't going for it, she may want to consider hyphenating her last name with yours. While putting two longer names together could sound a bit clunky, it may seem quite natural to combine two shorter names. If she has built an impressive professional reputation on her name, this may be a great way for her to retain the identity she has worked so hard to create. Another option is to consider legally changing her middle name to her maiden name instead and then taking her husband's last name. That way, she's still paying homage to her own family (which may be especially important to her if she's an only child), but your future children will still share your last name.

What's Required to Change Her Name

Your wife will need a certified copy of the marriage certificate in order to change her name. In most cases, she'll either need to appear in person or mail in copies of this certified document as well as bring or include at least two forms of personal identification. Check with each individual organization regarding its name-change policy.

Here are a few of the organizations she'll need to contact to change her last name:

- Department of Motor Vehicles (DMV)
- SSA
- Passport agency
- Her place of employment
- Banks
- Credit card companies
- Mortgage and lease holders
- Car title holders
- Utilities
- Insurance company
- Post office
- Voter's registration office

Wedding Insurance

Believe it or not, you can buy wedding insurance to cover your investment in your big day. Some venues may even require that you have wedding insurance in order to book a wedding with them.

Most insurance companies offer two different types of wedding insurance:

- Wedding event cancellation or postponement insurance covers lost deposits (for example, if your wedding must be cancelled due to a natural disaster, if one of your vendors goes out of business, if military leave isn't granted and the bride or groom can't make it to the wedding, or if an unexpected illness affects the bride or groom).

- Wedding liability insurance protects you from financial liability resulting from your wedding (such as if someone is injured in your reception hall).

Much like travel insurance for your honeymoon, in the event of a hurricane, flood, tornado, earthquake, or other natural disaster, a wedding event cancellation insurance policy will cover you. Additionally, your wedding policy will allow you to recover any prepaid deposits or additional expenses in the event that your reception venue closes, your DJ doesn't show up, your photographer doesn't deliver your photos, or your wedding cake shop burns down two weeks before your wedding. Some policies may also cover wedding gifts that are lost or stolen and replace wedding attire and jewelry that's lost or damaged.

With wedding liability insurance, you'll be covered in the event that you're held liable for bodily injury to any of your guests or for any property damage to your ceremony, reception, or rehearsal dinner venues. Liquor liability may also be available to cover any alcohol-related accidents.

As with other wedding vendors, you should thoroughly check out your insurer before signing anything. Ask them to spell out exactly what's covered in your policy and what isn't—and at what cost. Find out how soon you'd be reimbursed in the event of a claim. Last, make sure to ask for references from other clients in your area.

Vendor Contracts

It's very important to carefully review all your vendors' contracts before signing them so that you'll be aware of everything you're agreeing to and will know exactly what services to expect in exchange for the money you'll be paying.

MAN DOWN

Don't overlook reviewing the fine print in all of your wedding contracts. While reading vendor contracts may be about as exciting as watching paint dry, it pays to do your homework so you don't get caught with your pants down later on. Know exactly what you're paying for up front to make sure everyone's on the same page regarding expectations.

When reviewing contracts, here are a few general items to look out for:

- Does the contract include my name, my bride's name, and our planned wedding date?

- Does the contract spell out any specific time frames in which services will take place?

- Does the contract spell out exactly what services we'll be receiving and at what cost?

- Will services only be provided within certain hours?

- Are there any additional costs we'll incur for overtime or in the event that we must cancel or postpone the wedding?

- What will happen in the event of a vendor's equipment failure, illness, or other emergency on the day of the wedding?

- Is the vendor insured in case of equipment damage or loss?

Last, make sure that all parties sign on the dotted lines at the end of the contract to ensure that it's a legally binding agreement and will be recognized by a court of law. In the event that you have to pursue any legal actions down the line, a signed contract will give you a much sturdier leg to stand on.

Glossary

adventure bachelor party   A bachelor party held in a destination other than a bar or strip club. Popular activities include golfing, camping, and paintballing.

all-inclusives   Hotels, resorts, and cruises that charge a flat, per-person rate for accommodations, meals, and drinks as well as certain additional services and activities.

bling   Slang for sparkly jewelry, such as a diamond engagement ring.

bridezilla   An evil, Godzilla-like manifestation of your bride borne from the stress associated with wedding planning.

cash bar   A bar that lets wedding reception guests order drinks on their own dime. Some cash bars may charge guests for all alcoholic drinks or only charge for drinks made with top-tier liquors.

charity wedding registry   A gift registry that lets your friends and family contribute money to a specific cause in lieu of gifts.

co-ed bachelor(ette) party   A bachelor party that includes both male and female friends of the bride and groom.

couples shower   A co-ed wedding shower created around a theme that appeals to both the bride and groom.

create-a-gift registry   These registries can be set up through your bank or credit card issuer to allow guests to make cash contributions toward a big-ticket item, such as a house down payment.

cummerbund   A pleated waist sash often worn as an accessory to a tuxedo.

D.I.Y.   Do it yourself.

eco-friendly jewelry   Precious stones, such as diamonds, that are mined in ways that don't harm the environment or lead to violence and human rights abuses.

excursions   Extra off-site honeymoon activities (typically on a cruise), such as deep-sea fishing, helicopter tours, surfing lessons, dolphin watching, and mountain climbing.

first dance   The bride and groom's first dance together as a married couple. This is typically the first dance of the evening at the wedding reception, before the floor is opened for guests to join in.

groom's blogs   An increasingly popular way for grooms to share their wedding-planning stories and ideas on the Internet.

groom's cake   A smaller, secondary cake that focuses specifically on the groom's interests, such as his career, hobby, favorite sports team, or hometown.

groom's corner   An area set up at a wedding show to showcase the wedding vendors and businesses that grooms typically deal with directly.

groom's toast   A speech the groom is expected to deliver that focuses on the bride as well as families and guests, thanking them for their love and support. This toast is typically delivered at either the rehearsal dinner or wedding reception.

groomsmen gifts   Loot bestowed upon the best man, groomsmen, and other important ancillary positions to show appreciation for their involvement in the wedding.

honeymoon wedding registry   Instead of gifts, friends and family can use this registry to contribute cash donations toward the couple's honeymoon.

jewelry appraisal   A formal statement declaring the worth of a piece of jewelry.

man shower   A men-only shower where guys typically get together to eat, drink, and shoot the bull before the wedding and guests bring manly gifts for the groom.

marriage certificate   The certified document received after the wedding ceremony once the witnesses and officiant have all signed it and the officiant has sent it in to be recorded.

marriage license   A document applied for, purchased, and obtained, typically at the county's courthouse, in order to be legally married.

marriage prep   Required pre-wedding classes for the bride and groom that cover topics such as marital duties, planning for children, and finances.

no-play list   A list of songs to absolutely not play at the wedding reception (Prince's "Pussy Control," for example, may be a great club song but probably not for a wedding). Provide this list to the entertainer prior to the reception to ensure that even if someone requests them, they will not be played.

officiant   An ordained clergy member, judge, or justice who can legally perform wedding ceremonies.

prenup or prenuptial agreement   An agreement a couple makes prior to getting married in which they relinquish future rights to each other's property and assets in the event of divorce or death.

processional   The procession of your wedding party members walking down the aisle during the wedding ceremony.

save-the-dates   Cards that inform wedding guests about the upcoming wedding date and location so they can mark the date on their calendars. Formal wedding invitations are then sent later, closer to the wedding date.

setting   The method of securing a stone onto a piece of jewelry.

stag night   Another term for bachelor party.

the four Cs   The four pieces of criteria under which diamonds are graded: cut, color, clarity, and carat.

wedding event cancellation insurance   An insurance policy that covers lost wedding deposits due to unexpected reasons, such as weather, illness, and business closings.

wedding liability insurance   An insurance policy that protects couples from financial liability resulting from the wedding, such as personal injuries or property damage.

wife up   When a man decides to marry the smokin' hot woman who will become his wife.

wolf pack   A code name for the dudes in the wedding party that symbolizes the close bond shared with them.

B

Wedding Reception Playlist Ideas

Having a hard time choosing songs for your wedding reception playlist? Here are some popular selections—including classics and modern hits—to consider.

Newlyweds' First Dance

"Marry Me" by Train

"Lucky" by Jason Mraz and Colbie Caillat

"Forever" by Ben Harper

"Fly Me to the Moon" by Frank Sinatra

"Be Mine" by David Gray

"I Cross My Heart" by George Strait

"'Til Kingdom Come" by Coldplay

"Green Eyes" by Coldplay

"When You Say Nothing at All" by Alison Krause

"Come Away With Me" by Norah Jones

"Wild Horses" by The Rolling Stones

"Your Song" by Elton John

"Love Will Keep Us Alive" by The Eagles

"It Had To Be You" by Harry Connick Jr.

"The Way You Look Tonight" by Frank Sinatra

"Bless the Broken Road" by Rascal Flatts

"Better Together" by Jack Johnson

"By Your Side" by Sade

"At Last" by Etta James

"Wonderful Tonight" by Eric Clapton

"Amazed" by Lonestar

"Unforgettable" by Natalie & Nat King Cole

"One" by U2

"All I Want Is You" by U2

"Into the Mystic" by Van Morrison

"All My Life" by KC and JoJo

"When a Man Loves a Woman" by Percy Sledge

"The Greatest Fan of Your Life" by Edwin McCain

"The Luckiest" by Ben Folds

"Lost In This Moment" by Big & Rich

"I Finally Found Someone" by Barbra Streisand and Bryan Adams

Father-Daughter Dance

"My Girl" by The Temptations

"Daughters" by John Mayer

"I Loved Her First" by Heartland

"Butterfly Kisses" by Bob Carlisle

"My Little Girl" by Tim McGraw

"Isn't She Lovely" by Stevie Wonder

"You Are So Beautiful" by Joe Cocker

"How Sweet It Is (To Be Loved By You)" by James Taylor

"Because You Loved Me" by Celine Dion

Mother-Son Dance

"Somewhere Over the Rainbow" by Bernstein/Sondheim/Streisand

"My Wish" by Rascal Flatts

"I Hope You Dance" by Lee Ann Womack

"Because You Loved Me" by Celine Dion

"Have I Told You Lately" Rod Stewart

"Landslide" by Fleetwood Mac

"I Wish You Love" by Natalie Cole

Great Fast Songs for the Reception

"Love Shack" by The B52's

"Billie Jean" by Michael Jackson

"Sweet Caroline" by Neil Diamond

"Don't Stop Believin'" by Journey

"Pretty Woman" by Roy Orbison

"Brown-Eyed Girl" by Van Morrison

"You May Be Right" by Billy Joel

"Ants Marching" by The Dave Matthews Band

"Something to Talk About" by Bonnie Raitt

"Old Time Rock & Roll" by Bob Seger

"What I Like About You" by The Romantics

"Takin' Care of Business" by BTO

"Friends in Low Places" by Garth Brooks

"I Will Survive" by Gloria Gaynor

"Brick House" by The Commodores

"Get Down Tonight" by KC & The Sunshine Band

"Shout" by Otis Day & The Knights

"We Are Family" by Sister Sledge

"Long Train Running" by The Doobie Brothers

"September" by Earth, Wind, & Fire

"Stayin' Alive" by The Bee Gees

"Twist and Shout" by The Beatles

"Thriller" by Michael Jackson

"Oh What a Night" by The Four Seasons

"Canned Heat" by Jamiroquai

"Feel Good, Inc." by The Gorillaz

"White Wedding" by Billy Idol

"Ice Ice Baby" by Vanilla Ice

"Dancing Queen" by ABBA

"You Shook Me" by AC/DC

"Another One Bites the Dust" by Queen

"Sweet Home Alabama" by Lynyrd Skynyrd

"Margaritaville" by Jimmy Buffett

"Ring of Fire" by Johnny Cash

"Livin' on a Prayer" by Bon Jovi

"Sweet Child of Mine" by Guns 'n' Roses

"Footloose" by Kenny Loggins

"Respect" by Aretha Franklin

"Take on Me" by A-Ha

Great Slow Songs for the Reception

"Young Forever" by Jay-Z

"Forever Young" by Alphaville

"What a Wonderful World" by Louis Armstrong

"Imagine" by John Lennon

"Unchained Melody" by The Righteous Brothers

"Stand by Me" by Sam Cooke

"Let's Stay Together" by Al Green

"From This Moment" by Shania Twain

"It's Your Love" by Tim McGraw & Faith Hill

"Take My Breath Away" by Berlin

"You've Lost That Lovin' Feeling" by The Righteous Brothers

"Time After Time" by Cyndi Lauper

"Can't Help Falling in Love" by Elvis Presley

"Moondance" by Van Morrison

"In Your Eyes" by Peter Gabriel

"I Don't Want to Miss a Thing" by Aerosmith

"I've Had the Time of my Life" by Bill Medley & Jennifer Warnes

Bachelor Party Challenges

One of your best man's key jobs is to plan and execute a bachelor party that will give you a proper send-off into married life. If your dream stag night consists of hitting the bars, casinos, or strip clubs, it's never a bad idea to have a list of challenges or games for you and your bros to complete during the course of the night. When telling the best man what style of party you want, be sure to let him know that you'd like as much debauchery as possible. If properly planned, these challenges can turn into some hilarious moments that won't soon be forgotten:

- The groom must get 50 women to sign his shirt.
- Stuff a fanny pack full of embarrassing, random items. Make the groom wear it around all night until he has given all the bag's contents to women.
- Find a girl with the same name as your fiancée and buy her a drink.
- Find 10 girls who smoke and offer each of them a light.
- Get the best man's phone number into 10 random girls' phones.

- Get a woman's bra.

- Get a woman's underwear.

- Get a woman's phone number.

- Find a woman on her bachelorette party and make the groom dance with her.

- Do a body shot off a woman.

- Have a woman do a body shot off the groom.

- Make the groom carry an inflatable doll around all night.

- Get a blonde, a brunette, and a red-head to each buy the groom a drink.

- Serenade an unsuspecting girl with a love song.

- Make the groom wear a ball and chain around all night.

- For every beer or drink the groom gets, make him ask for a girl's phone number. Every time he gets shot down, he has to take a shot.

- Find a woman who can tie a cherry stem into a knot with her tongue. Make her prove it, then buy her a drink.

- Have the groom find a girl with really bright lipstick to kiss his cheek. Don't let him wash it off all night.

- Have a girl do a naughty dance move for the groom for a drink or beads.

- Convince a girl to rub the best man's shoulders.

- Try to convince a woman that women should remain virgins until marriage and that men shouldn't have to.

Remember to keep score to see how many the groom can complete. Here's the official The Man Registry scoring breakdown for the groom:

0–5: *Are you already married?*

6–12: *Maybe a couple more years of bachelorhood wouldn't be a bad thing.*

13–20: *Time to cut off the booze.*

21: *Maybe marriage isn't the best idea for you.*

The Groom's Wedding-Day Attire Checklist

Your wedding day will be one of the most important days of your life. Will you be nervous about looking your best? Of course. You can try to play it off cool, but on a day like this—when wedding guests, photographers, and your bride will be coming at you from every direction—it's only natural to be a little self-conscious.

How can you curb your worries? Two words: be prepared (just like that old Cub Scout motto). It's extremely helpful to plan all the details before the ceremony so you can enjoy your wedding day without worrying about whether you smell or whether you have something stuck in your teeth. To make sure you have everything you could possibly need to look your best on your big day, take a look at our groom's wedding-day checklist.

Attire—Don't Forget

- Tux or suit basics (pants, shirt, and jacket)
- Cummerbund or vest
- Tie
- Socks (that match your shoes)
- Shoes
- Cuff links and watch
- Sunglasses

Before Leaving for the Church

- Shower
- Put on deodorant
- Brush your teeth, floss, and gargle with mouthwash
- Trim your nails
- Shave
- Take any prescribed medication or allergy pills
- If wearing cologne, gently apply it

- Make sure the groom or best man has the bride's wedding ring and any gifts that are needed at ceremony site or reception

Emergency Kit: Just in Case

- Eye drops
- Band-Aids
- Sunscreen
- Bug spray
- Duct tape (never leave home without it)
- Lint roller
- Extra socks and undershirt
- Hair gel
- Shoe polish
- Wedding party contact information
- Safety pins

Additional Resources

Here's a quick rundown of some useful URLs you can visit to enhance your wedding-planning experience:

The Man Registry Network of Sites

Create a guy-friendly gift registry:
www.themanregistry.com

Browse our collection of thousands of unique groomsmen gifts with free shipping on larger orders:
www.themanregistry.com/gifts/groomsmen-gifts

Read articles and print checklists that give you the goods on wedding planning, timelines, and duties:
www.themanregistry.com/groom101

Search your city or region for wedding vendors in categories such as entertainment, transportation, attire, and bachelor party venues:
www.themanregistry.com/vendors

Read or subscribe to our blog that's updated daily and offers an offbeat look at groom's style and wedding culture from a man's perspective: **www.groomsadvice.com**

Real Groom Bloggers

There's no better way to learn something than by studying those who have gone before you. Check out these blogs written by real grooms:

The Groom Says
www.thegroomsays.blogspot.com

Temple of Groom
www.templeofgroom.blogspot.com

Ben the Groom
www.benthegroom.com

Start a Free Wedding Blog

Inspired by all the great wedding blogs out there? Well, what are you waiting for? Start your own blog today by visiting one of these free sites. If you're a programming whiz, you can also purchase your own domain and build a site from scratch. Who knows, maybe you'll end up guest blogging for The Man Registry!

www.wordpress.com

www.blogger.com

www.tumbler.com